SCAVENGERS

A True Story of Money, Madness and Murder

BY D

RIVERVIEWBOOKS LLC

Printed in the United States of America

ISBN: 978-0-615-49491-3

Library of Congress Control Number: 2011909366

Photo credits: Courtesy Indianapolis Star for Jackson residence, courtroom; other photos courtesy of the Marion County Sheriff's Department.

Contact: Riverview Books LLC, P.O. Box 30208, Indianapolis IN 46230 or Riverviewbooks.com

Cast of Characters

VICTIMS

Lafayette Andrew Jackson, grocery chain founder, gunned down in robbery.
Chester Jackson, his son, robbery and extortion victim.
Marjorie Jackson, Chester's widow, murder victim.

KILLERS

Charles Vernon Witt, escaped from prison after killing deputy sheriff.
Louis Hamilton, parole violator, Witt's confederate.
Howard Russell Willard, ex-convict, burglar.

ACCOMPLICES

Emanuel Robinson, ex-convict, burglar.
Marjorie Pollitt, Willard's wife and girlfriend.

OTHER SCAVENGERS

John Alton Williams, inner-city car wash owner who accepted stolen money from Robinson.
Herbert D. Biddle, Jr., banker whose embezzling caused Marjorie Jackson to withdraw $8 million cash.
Jerry Hornick, former divinity student who hatched a burglary plan and chain of events leading to murder.
Wally Bergin, high school dropout who committed initial burglary.
Walter Bergin, Sr., Wally's father, who found and hid stolen money.
Doug Green, Wally's partner, split more than $800,000 cash.
Judy Parrish, Green's sister kept stolen money hidden in her closet.

Gary Perkins, burglars' friend who said he could launder stolen money in Las Vegas.

Gary Walters, neophyte inventor went on a spending spree with Wally Bergin.

Ralph Wadsworth II, Indianapolis city employee tried to break into Jackson home.

Annie Young, inner-city welfare recipient had $957,619 in her apartment.

Robertina Harroll, Marjorie Pollitt's sister bought motor home with stolen money.

LAW ENFORCEMENT

Sgt. Harold Young, found trash barrel with $5,000,000 cash.

Sgt. Harlan Rynard, traced luxury car purchases.

Sgt. Dave Paschall, directed a dragnet for thieves and recipients of stolen money.

FBI agent Lee Mannen, the only "outsider" money-hoarding widow would trust.

Tommy Thompson, received the first tip about a major crime the victim refused to prosecute.

James F. Kelley, Indianapolis prosecutor who presented evidence against Jackson killers.

Steve Backer, Kelly's assistant in trial.

Aaron Haith, prosecutor spearheaded second trial.

John Schwartz, also prosecuted second trial.

DEFENSE ATTORNEYS

Jim Voyles, tried to keep his client from talking.

F. Lee Bailey, Boston attorney met fugitives in the desert.

Henry Gonzalez, Miami attorney served as co-counsel for Voyles.

Arnold Baratz, public defender fought murder conviction.

PROLOGUE

IN THE WITCH'S HOUSE

The belief in a supernatural source of
evil is unnecessary; men alone are quite
capable of every wickedness.

Joseph Conrad

SHE sealed off the outside world, for she
believed demons were everywhere. She allowed the
bushes and grass in her yard to grow unchecked. She
kept the gates in the chain-wire fence locked and
never opened the heavy pink drapes in the front room
nor the curtains and shades in the other five rooms.
To prevent devils from penetrating her sanctuary, she
covered vents, window cracks and door handles with
aluminum foil.

God and Jesus and his mother would have no
trouble getting in, when they came. And she knew
they would come. She prepared everything for their
visit. In one bedroom she covered the bed with fine
satin linen, and on the table next to the bed she put
small foil packages containing jewel-studded rings,
necklaces and watches. In each of these she wrote a

name, so there could be no confusion. "To God, from Marjorie." "To Jesus, from Marjorie." "To Holy Mother Merry."

Then, in the dining room, she laid out her finest silverware with plates and Ruby glass goblets. Next to each she placed more foil packages containing rings, watches, diamonds or pearls, each with its own note similar to the ones in the bedroom. In a few of them she placed new, carefully wrapped Cannon washcloths and gently sealed them shut. At each setting she placed fresh fruit, and did not notice when its flesh had rotted.

She was quite mad, of course, but no one who saw her on her occasional forays outside her protected domain on Spring Mill Road could tell from her appearance. In her mid-sixties, she had silver hair, fluffed out like cotton candy, and her makeup was always carefully applied. She wore expensive jewelry and furs, and never drove anything other than a Cadillac. She looked exactly like what she was not, a rich widow ready to dress down a caterer for delivering the wrong brand of caviar. In fact, money—and she had millions hidden all over the house—meant nothing to her.

She only ventured out between noon on Sundays and dusk on Tuesdays. The remainder of the time was dedicated to her devotions, including prayer sessions which went on for hours, marked by fervent recitations of the Scripture she knew by heart. With few friends and no relatives she trusted, her outings primarily were for shopping. All purchases had one purpose, to help prepare the house for Armageddon.

Each week she filled her Cadillac with bags of food, dozens of loaves of bread, boxes of cookies and cereal, canned goods almost beyond count. Her kitchen had so much food—150 pounds of coffee, for example—there was hardly room for her to cook. She wanted to have everything she possibly would need for that time after He descended from the heavens and raised the dead from their graves. Thus, she had fifty pairs of pajamas.

Each week, too, she bought fresh flowers. At her favorite little shop, in the Broad Ripple district of Indianapolis, she usually selected fresh-cut roses. She paid for these with crisp old $20 or $50 Federal Reserve notes, many printed in Philadelphia in 1932, which were worth four or five times their face value. She always refused the change. When the friendly young clerks asked her where she got her money, she laughed, "Oh, I just grow it in the ground. I touch the earth and money comes out."

And this was how a certain band of predators came to believe the woman was a witch.

This belief was the seed for the theft of $3,800,000, the largest cash burglary in American history. Some would whisper that the family fortune carried a curse, for over a forty-six year period it lured twenty-four people into crime and brought about two murders and two executions by electrocution.

Alone in that strange house, like a silver-wigged Bette Davis in a Gothic movie, she played her organ and piano for hours on end, sang songs to herself, read her Bible, and made her preparations. She felt protected from the devils, and waited for the inevitable knock on the door that would signal the beginning of her salvation for all the sins of the past.

1: THE KILLERS

L. A. JACKSON owned two hundred and twenty-six grocery stores. It was a cash business, drawing in several hundred thousand dollars a day, and a tempting target in these lawless times. Single-handedly, he had built up a multi-million dollar empire, and the only way anybody would steal his money, even a dollar, would be over his dead body.

Lafayette Andrew Jackson's stubborn pledge proved to be a prophecy.

People who read of his defiance as reported in the Indianapolis *Star* one morning in 1931 could sense the certainty in L.A. Jackson's words. The owner of the Standard Grocery chain opined: "Criminals get off too easy nowadays. If anybody pokes a gun at me, I'm going to let him have it. Maybe I'll get killed, but I've got to die sometime. Even if I am shot, I can still shoot."

L.A. was sixty-eight. He was a large, somewhat round man, with dark, owlish eyebrows over thick-framed glasses on an oval face, thinning silver hair, and prominent ears. A gold tooth flashed when he spoke. Usually he wore conservative suits, bow ties, and, occasionally, garters to hold up his sleeves. In a pigeonhole in his desk at the company's main office near the stone and brick heart of downtown, he kept a Colt six-shooter. The revolver was always there, just as the desk lamp signaled when the owner wasn't. No employee was allowed to light the lamp when L.A. was away.

The lamp symbolized his legendary frugality. The revolver symbolized his resolve.

Anyone who saw the man striding determinedly along Washington Street, the Hoosier capital's main east-west thoroughfare, might wonder if he were an evangelizing preacher. He carried himself with the stamp of a fellow who had something to say and little time to waste in the doing. Which was exactly how he had built up the largest chain of grocery stores serving the area's 417,000 residents.

People who knew L.A. didn't doubt that he would defend a handful of pennies just as resolutely as he would defend all of his fortune, and not just because police headquarters was less than three blocks from Standard's main office at 419 E. Washington. He was one of those single-minded, self-made mercantilists, born in the nineteenth century, who boasted that he never took a day of vacation. It was not unusual for him to work until midnight and to be the first behind his desk in the morning. If plow-horse work habits made him rich, he had his idiosyncrasies. Although he was friend and confidant of the city's banking families, he distrusted banks and feared tax collectors. He kept part of his own fortune in cash, hidden at home.

In a sense, the money he made was less important than the process of earning it. In a sense, too, a million dollars was no more important than a wad of singles. L.A. would fight equally hard for both; it was a matter of principle. He liked to say his principles owed something to the blood of Old Hickory that pulsed in his veins, though the genealogical chain taking him back to President Andrew Jackson lacked a few links.

From his Kentucky hill country roots and the genes of his Jackson forebears, he drew faith in Yankee capitalism and dour piety bed-rocked in a Christianity shorn of fancy ornamentation. Bath County, where he was born during the Civil War, was a place to leave. Located on the hilly fringes of the rich blue grass region in northeastern Kentucky, the area had few people and fewer opportunities; the population of the entire county would always hover around ten thousand.

The only question was where the young man would go after he finished his schooling and made up his mind to carve out a career in retailing. The advertisement in a Cincinnati newspaper settled matters. Barney H. Kroger needed salesmen to help in his new Kroger Grocery and Baking Co. as it spread out through the 1880s. In Lafayette Jackson, Mr. Kroger would see a "bright, energetic and go-ahead type of chap."

In 1891 the twenty-eight year old Kroger
employee set out on his own. With wife, Mamie, and
young son Chester, he made his way to the Railroad
City of Indianapolis and opened a small grocery store
on Washington Street. The Indiana capital was a
perfect location for a conservative, no-nonsense,
hard-working white man who took time on Sundays
to worship the Christian god. It was not just a
growing town where America's mighty railroads
converged only a handful of miles from the
population center of the U.S.; Indianapolis was
considered the geographical center of American
manufacturing. L.A. soon began adding about one
store a year. By 1910 he had twenty-one.

His willingness to work long hours accounted
for much of his success. His flexibility helped; he
would write deals on the backs of envelopes. His
stinginess didn't hurt; he would argue with salesmen
over expenses and warn his employees not to waste
electricity. The Standard grocery signs became familiar
in and around the capital. In 1929, the governor of his
home state recognized his achievement with an
honorary appointment as a Kentucky Colonel.

On the rare occasions away from work, L.A.
liked to revisit the scenes of his childhood. He'd take
his family on a train to Lexington and drive a rented
buggy to the rugged back country. Besides Chester,
Lafayette and Mamie produced a second son,
Howard, and a daughter, Charlotte. When Mamie died
prematurely, in 1896, L.A. at least had the means to
hire others to help raise the little ones. Then he met a

pretty art student also named Jackson, Edith Elizabeth Jackson, and married her. They had a daughter, Marguerite. Edith was a frail woman with a frail heart. In the latter part of the marriage she was invalided for long periods. She was only in her fifties when she died, in 1928.

The father made the grocery business a family affair. Chester grew up learning the trade. Although weakened by childhood polio, Howard went to work with them when he was old enough. Marguerite married Ed Wiest, a Standard executive and one of L.A.'s trusted assistants.

Wiest perhaps epitomized his father-in-law's resolve. In 1927, at one of the Standard stores north of downtown, Wiest came upon two men pulling a robbery. They responded with bullets. For sixteen weeks he lay near death, before rebounding and recovering completely. In his office at company headquarters, Ed kept a teargas gun.

L.A.'s revolver had real bullets. "They'll never take anything from me," he pledged. "I'll shoot first."

It was the kind of talk the newspapers would describe as his "fighting spirit."

The phrase was remembered in an editorial which was published the same day as L.A.'s obituary.

SOME time during the damp spring that gave no hint of the hot parched summer of 1931 to come, two strangers arrived in Indianapolis.

They were anonymous faces who avoided attention and could avoid attention because in these hard times, anonymous faces came by the hundreds, by bus, car or any of the one hundred and sixty-five passenger trains that arrived or departed Union Station daily. The depression that had strangled many of the nation's farms since the early part of the 1920s had leaped into the towns and cities in the new decade. Nearly twelve million people were out of work. A stream of transients went from town to town, city to city, in hopes the next stop would have something better than the one before.

Indianapolis had been hurt but not, as yet, as hard as some cities. People with a little money in their pockets could get by here. For fifty cents the Roberts Restaurant served up a complete chicken dinner or its prime rabbit dinner. Men could buy one of Crane's Imported Cigars for a nickel. The big Block's department store sold men's shirts for as low as $1.15. All-steel iceboxes could be purchased for $25.50, and prices were starting to drop for the new electric-powered "refrigerators." The Pearson Piano Co. advertised radios, "complete with tubes," for $39. A good used car could be bought for under $100, and for those still on the wave of prosperity, the sleek Auburn Phaeton Sedan was available for $1,145. A police "crackdown" suggested the city's notorious gambling dens were doing good business.

These two men preferred anonymity for their own reasons. Both were wanted by the law.

The 1930s were a time we look back upon as a kind of black and white newsreel, and in the old black and white photos Charles Vernon Witt stares at the camera with an air of dusky insolence. Twenty-five, Witt had lazy dark eyes, high forehead, aquiline nose, and thick dark hair parted on the left. His ears were slightly crooked, as if he wore his hat too low. Born on a small hardscrabble farm less than an hour's drive west of Indianapolis, he had had a high school education and claimed to be a toolmaker by trade.

In reality he was a criminal. From his teens he had been a suspect or defendant in a variety of offenses. Robbery became his specialty. In 1927 he was caught and convicted of killing a deputy sheriff in rural western Kansas. Sentenced to life in prison, Witt had served three years before escaping from the Kansas State Penitentiary just before Christmas 1930. He had another reason for keeping a low-profile in Indianapolis. He was a fugitive on an old indictment for the robbery of a local woman.

Six months younger, Louis Hamilton had a boyish complexion and easy good looks. His oval face with a low pointy chin and thin eyebrows sat under wavy brown hair receding on the left side. He was a small man, only five foot seven and a half inches tall, only a hundred and thirty-two pounds. Born in Kansas of parents who had once lived near Indianapolis, Hamilton began getting in trouble at a young age, much to the perplexity of his father, a respected Iola insurance and real estate man who followed a religious movement called Millennial

Divinity. At eighteen Louis got his first hard sentence, eighteen months in reform school for assault with intent to kill. In 1926 he was arrested and sentenced to five-to-fifteen years for vehicle theft.

Prison was where he met Witt. While Witt was wanted as a dangerous escapee, Hamilton was sought for violating his parole. Not long after his release from prison in June 1930, he simply disappeared from official sight.

When the two men arrived in Indianapolis they knew where to go. They rented upstairs rooms in a house in a quiet tree-lined neighborhood. Their landlord was a man named Milo Stockberger, who was known to some people as a bookkeeper and to others as a bootlegger. Stockberger introduced the new arrivals to his ex-wife Naomi, a willowy redhead who was known as Babe.

Later Stockberger would claim Hamilton and Witt invited him to join them in robbing the headquarters of the Standard chain, where the cash receipts from all the stores were collected and the armored car supposedly didn't arrive to pick up the money until ten o'clock.

On the morning of May 27, 1931, the lights went on early as usual at Standard Grocery's combination headquarters, branch store and warehouse in a limestone and brick building just east of downtown, only two and a half blocks from police headquarters and the ancient Marion County Jail.

After a period of cool intermittent showers the weather had started to warm into the low eighties. It was a good omen for the annual "500" race three days hence, which Billy Arnold had won last year by averaging the breakneck speed of one hundred miles an hour for only the second time. All the news from the qualifying trials in neighboring Speedway wasn't so good; driver Joe Caccia and his mechanic were killed when he hit the wall in the southwest turn. Still, the race was a big Memorial Day weekend attraction, and merchants were sprucing up the town.

On this Wednesday there was plenty of activity besides the race. Indiana's Masons were holding their largest convention ever. The Duesenberg automobile plant on the west side of town would open its doors for free public tours. Movie houses had lowered ticket prices to summer rates, a quarter to forty cents, and the Apollo had one of the top attractions, James Cagney playing a vicious gangster in *Public Enemy*.

Just after nine o'clock, a black Oldsmobile touring car, stolen earlier from the nearby community of Shelbyville, stopped at the curb, facing east, in front of the Standard building, and two men emerged.

Slowly they studied the street and the traffic. There were few cars as yet moving up and down the four lane pavement of asphalt and older brick, streaked with the tracks of the interurban line still in use. On the other side of the street were two businesses, two restaurants, apartments and an upstairs hotel. On this side, the Standard side, the Tremont Hotel stood on the farthest corner, the Gayety Theater next door was not yet open, and there were two other businesses, a men's clothing store and a distributor of furnace equipment. People were moving about, though not in great numbers.

The short man wore a brown suit, long striped gray overcoat, and a Panama hat with a black band, pulled down close to his eyes. The taller man, though he was under six feet, wore a dark suit. One had a sawed-off shotgun. The second carried a revolver.

Inside the office, L.A. Jackson, his son, Chester, son-in-law Ed Wiest, and half a dozen employees were following their routine morning schedule. A minute later, all hell broke loose.

The man with the shotgun stood near the door while the other man walked up to Chester Jackson. In a menacing but not especially loud voice, he demanded:

"Give me all the money."

"Don't fire," Chester said. "Be calm. I'll get you the money. It's in the safe."

L.A. looked up. "What's up, son?"

Exactly what happened next wasn't clear. In the blur of a moment L.A. kept his word, grabbing his revolver and firing once, but one of the gunmen may have got off the first shot. Then the closest yelled, "Let him have it!" A barrage of bullets erupted, followed by a brief silence.

"Don't shoot any more!" Chester yelled. "I'll open the safe and give you the money."

It was too late. Already the men were backing out the door.

Across the street, Police Detective Charles Bauer had heard the sound of gunfire and sprinted with revolver drawn in the direction of the Oldsmobile. Dozens of shots crackled. Bauer's bullets ripped a half-dozen holes in the car. A hail of fire from the gunmen sent him to the ground. Two other policemen who happened along unleashed more bullets. The car raced away.

Inside the business, L.A. stumbled into a washroom and wiped blood from his forehead. Then he collapsed.

Despite the chaos, this is how one witness was quoted in the newspaper:

"When I heard the shots I rushed outside and saw the detective walking along. He halted, saw where the trouble was, and, drawing his revolver, rushed toward the door of the store. A fusillade of gunfire met him, and, clutching his head with his left hand and still shooting his own revolver, he fell to his knee...Bauer was in a crossfire between the bandits inside and the fellow who was at the automobile. I never saw such courage and public spirit as that officer showed. In the face of overwhelming odds he had the nerve to tackle that gang when he didn't have a chance."

Bauer survived his wound. L.A. was semi-conscious by the time an ambulance arrived to take him to St. Vincent Hospital, where doctors discovered one bullet had damaged his head and another had gone clean through his abdomen. The sixty-eight year old merchant kept breathing for thirty-six hours. Just before he died he told his surgeon, "They shot me down like a dog."

Many of the city's prominent citizens turned out for the funeral. The brazenness of the stickup attempt, within "a stone's throw of police headquarters," caused the Indianapolis *Star* to write: "The boldness of the modern highwayman indicates his supreme contempt for the law and its agencies." The afternoon *News* lamented, "He died a victim of the inefficiency of a social organization which somehow is not able to protect life and property."

The rival afternoon paper, the *Times*, trumpeted the death of a crusader:

"While thousands whose benefit was his last predominant passion paid their last respects around the bier, in flesh and memory ranged a more intimate group who clung to his friendship through the years, like lesser flakes of metal to a giant magnet. They saw stifled the dynamo that thundered its way to power. They saw inert the hands that had in one minute driven a merciless bargain and in the next spread lavishly what calm they could to deliquesce all human ill. They saw liberated from the flesh the fighting spirit that fired the human machine, the spirit that urged him to a death that he had foreseen, as a crusader against a vicious enemy (crime) with the odds piled high against him."

Lafayette Andrew Jackson was buried in Crown Hill Cemetery, the city's largest. Here, three years later, the body of a Hoosier who symbolized the rampant crime of the era would be interred. His name was John Herbert Dillinger.

POLICE found the bullet-riddled Oldsmobile abandoned about six blocks away shortly after the bungled holdup.

The windshield was shattered. Blood was on the left running board, the left door handle, and the front seat, meaning at least one of the three robbers had been wounded. But were there three? The witnesses weren't sure. Certainly there were two.

Mayor Reginald Sullivan ordered an all-out police investigation. For weeks nothing happened beyond false leads and the release of hundreds of fliers with sketches of the wanted men. The police were busy questioning and threatening a network of informants in the city's criminal underworld. Were these local thugs or outsiders? If they were outsiders, they knew a lot about their target. In these cash-strapped times they had found a place with as much cash as a bank but without a bank's armed protection. Just a sixty-eight year old man whose reflexes weren't as fast as his resolve.

On June 25, as a heat wave fell over the city, a squad of police stopped a car a half-mile north of downtown and arrested Charles Witt before he could reach a loaded .45 in his shoulder holster. Witt insisted he had no part in any robbery. The officers noticed he had an unhealed wound in his hip. "Oh, that?" Witt said. "I got that a long time ago." Witt said his own gun had discharged accidentally.

At the rooming house, detectives arrested Witt's wife, Babe, as a material witness. She told them they had married on May 28 and she thought his last name was Irwin.

At headquarters, Witt was brought into a room where Chester Jackson and Detective Bauer could see him. Both identified him as one of the gunmen.

That same day, in tiny Iola, Kansas, police arrested Louis Hamilton as he prepared to go on his honeymoon. Hamilton's bride of thirteen hours insisted Hamilton couldn't have been in Indianapolis robbing a grocery chain on May 27 because he was with her and other family members, in Iola for her brother's birthday. "I'll stand by you, darling," she promised. "I know you're innocent." When Chester Jackson arrived in Iola at the request of the police, he said he thought Hamilton was the other gunman.

At police headquarters, detectives had an interrogation room known as the Black Hole of Calcutta. On the day after Witt's arrest, police emerged from the Black Hole with what they described as a voluntary signed confession. Officers assured reporters Witt had simply folded under skilled and intensive interrogation. The statement said:

On the morning of May 27, about nine a.m., I met Louis Hamilton at Massachusetts avenue and East street. Hamilton was in an Oldsmobile sedan where I expected to meet him, but did not expect him to have a car. I got in the car with Hamilton and while riding he suggested we stick up a Standard grocery store. Hamilton told me there was a double-barreled sawed-off shotgun in the back seat of the car and for me to use it.

When we got to the Standard Grocery store on East Washington near New Jersey he stopped the car in front and told me to follow him. I then took the shotgun out of the car and followed Hamilton into the store. After we were in the store Hamilton told me to cover those people. Hamilton then started through a door into the office. I heard several shots fired in the office and Hamilton called to me to "Let them have it."

I fired one shot toward the rear of the store. I then turned around as a man came in the front door shooting at me. I fired one shot at him. I meant to hit him in the legs. I called to Hamilton to "Come on, let's go."

We left the store and got into the automobile parked in front. As I started to get in someone shot me in the left leg. Hamilton drove the car east and while riding I noticed that Hamilton had been shot in the forehead. We drove to the neighborhood of Twelfth and Illinois where we left the car and walked back to Tenth and Park, where I had my car parked. Hamilton and I got in my car and drove to my parents' home near Bainbridge, Ind., where I picked up my wife Naomi and the three of us went on to Iola to the home of Louis Hamilton.

My wife and I spent a few days with Hamilton and his folks and then we left, returning to my parents' home, where I left my wife. Then I went to Terre Haute, where I disposed of the Chrysler sedan I had been driving and took a bus to Richmond, Ind., where I bought a Ford sedan. Then I went and got my wife and took a trip through the East. We then returned to Indianapolis, where I was arrested. I make this statement of my own free will and accord.

Witt's alleged statement raised as many questions as it answered. His claim that Hamilton was the mastermind seemed to pale when the old robbery indictment against Witt was dug out. Next, a rural grocery store owner identified Witt as the man who had robbed him, and, in Iola, witnesses identified photos of Witt as the man who had robbed a savings and loan just a few weeks earlier.

Two days later, back in Indianapolis, detectives took Hamilton into the Black Hole. It was 98 degrees outside and hotter inside. When they came out, Hamilton was unshaven and looked haggard. Detectives waved a signed confession. It differed significantly from Witt's version:

On May 22, 1931, Charles Vernon Witt and myself drove to Shelbyville, Ind., in Witt's Chrysler car, where we stole an Oldsmobile coach and drove it back to Indianapolis. I do not remember who drove it back. We then drove it around the streets of Indianapolis. We parked it in a shed, but I do not know the street or address, but it was near where I was rooming.

About May 25, 1931, Charles Vernon Witt and myself talked about sticking up the main store of the Standard grocery, as we were informed that an armored car came to the Standard grocery about ten o'clock in the mornings for money.

On May 27, 1931, Charles Vernon Witt and myself went to the shed where he had the Oldsmobile coach and I drove to the main store of the Standard grocery on east Washington. I entered the store first and Witt followed me. I had a .45 automatic pistol and Witt had a sawed-off shotgun. I went to the office where there were about four or five men sitting behind a cage. I pointed my gun at these men, none in particular, and at the same time remarked, "Stick 'em up and give me the money." At this time I was struck with a bullet in the forehead but I do not know who fired the shot. I did see a man standing behind the cage with a gun in his hand. I heard a number of shots fired but I do not remember how many I fired. I do remember I had a clip containing eight bullets in the gun and I reloaded with a clip containing eight bullets before I left the store.

After I was struck in the forehead I was dazed and could not remember how many shots I fired.

We left the store together. I entered the car first and Witt followed. I drove the car away from the store. After driving a few squares Witt took the wheel as my head was bleeding freely. I got in the back of the car. I do not remember where we left the car as I was still in a dazed condition. I did not come to myself until I was riding in a Chrysler car towards Witt's father's home. Witt, Naomi and myself left Witt's father's house on the 27th of May about 4 p.m. and drove to my mother's home in Iola, Kan., arriving on May 28 about 5 p.m. The gun I used in the Jackson stickup I threw in the river while driving to my home in Iola, Kan. There was no one in on the Jackson stickup except Charles Vernon Witt and myself.

I make this statement of my own free will and accord.

Babe Witt wiped her eyes with a tissue as she talked to a reporter at headquarters under the watchful eye of a police matron. The reporter would quote her as saying:

"Just say this for me—whether you put anything else in the paper or not—put this in and be sure and get it straight, that I'll stick to that man to the electric chair. Why? Because I love him that much. I loved him when I married him. I love him yet. And if ever a man needs his woman, he needs me now. He's in a jam, and I'll stick if I have to go to the chair, too."

Finally brought into a packed courtroom, Witt seemed cool and calm. He insisted the confession was phony. "That's a lot of bunk," he declared for all to hear. "I didn't make any statement and I didn't sign any paper." Hamilton followed suit; he had made no "confession" because he had nothing to confess.

With the two alleged killers now safely in the Marion County Jail, feelings ran high in Indianapolis, exacerbated as thermostats boiled towards one hundred degrees day after unrelenting day. When Hamilton's wife and relatives from Kansas tried to visit him, the sheriff, "Buck" Sumner, argued with defense attorney Ira Holmes in front of the jail to the point where they had to be separated. "He hit me with a blackjack without warning," Holmes told reporters. Sumner fired back: "When I need a blackjack to handle guys like that, I'll quit." Holmes filed a $25,000 lawsuit against the sheriff. Sumner had to cancel an appearance in a golf outing because of a bruised knuckle. He couldn't grip his clubs properly.

Publicity and animosity aside, Holmes faced a formidable pile of evidence. In addition, the state wanted a speedy trial, and the state would get what it wanted.

For the moment the best Holmes could do was to demand separate trials and seek a change of venue from the vigilante climate of Marion County. He succeeded on both counts. His clients would be tried, Witt first, in adjoining Boone County. At least there would be the advantage of a jury not poisoned by the intense newspaper coverage in Indianapolis.

There also would be a disadvantage. The jury would be largely made up of farmers who, in spite of claims of impartiality, would be fearful of greedy outsiders willing to kill to get money. And in Indiana, a conviction for murder in the commission of a robbery automatically carried the death penalty.

When the Witt trial started in January 1932 in the Courthouse in nearby Lebanon, Holmes had to be less confident than Prosecutor Ben Scifres. Although the jury included housewives and professional men as well as farmers, the judge approved the prosecution's request to have Witt shackled, since he was an escaped murderer. Besides this, the old courtroom was packed from day one. A big murder trial involving desperadoes was an event. Kids playing hooky from school joined their elders in squeezing into every seat. So many people clambered inside, the judge finally had to clear the aisles and rope off the back row.

In the six days of evidence, rebuttal and argument, Holmes won one important victory. Impressed by the defense's contention that the defendant had been worked over with a blackjack, Judge John Hornaday threw out Witt's confession. Otherwise, the state's case was strong, especially the testimony of three Standard employees, and Detective Bauer, identifying Witt as one of the bandits.

Perhaps just as damaging was the surprise testimony of landlord Milo Stockberger. Among other things he placed Witt and Hamilton together and said they had a .45 automatic like the one that killed L.A.

Jackson. On the day of the robbery, Stockberger said, the pair came to his house claiming they'd been involved in a raid at a still but then admitting the Standard job. The best Holmes could do was identify Babe Witt, sitting near her husband in the courtroom, as Stockberger's former wife, and attack his testimony as that of a vengeful, jealous man.

Once the prosecution rested, Holmes fought back. He presented six of Hamilton's relatives, all testifying that Mr. and Mrs. Witt had been attending a birthday party in Iola on the day of the robbery attempt. Scifres came back with rebuttal witnesses, including a woman who claimed the Witts and Hamilton showed up on May 28, not May 27.

The prosecutor had a strong hole card. He called Chester Jackson. The young grocer offered powerful testimony about seeing his father murdered. He identified Hamilton as the man who shot L.A., and named Witt as his accomplice.

The final arguments were as impassioned as the publicity about the case. The jury retired, and returned with its verdict: guilty of murder.

Six days later, Witt stood blank-faced in front of the judge, who announced: "Before the hour of sunrise on Aug, 1, 1932, the warden of the state prison shall take Charles Vernon Witt into a room arranged for said purpose and there put him to death." Witt shrugged. "I'd rather get what I got here than have to go back to the Kansas state prison," he said.

Witt was transported to the state prison near Michigan City, in northwestern Indiana, and locked in Death Row. The electric chair, known as Hot Squat, waited in a nearby room. It was an ugly contraption constructed out of the scaffolding originally used to hang inmates. The state had switched to electrocution in 1913, and usually executed one or two inmates each year, normally without fanfare. Indiana was the first state to adapt iron rods in place of leather straps to hold the prisoner in place. Witt could appeal his conviction, but in this era, appeals were resolved much faster than they would be in the second half of the century.

Predators weren't quite finished with Chester Jackson.

One afternoon, the new president of Standard Grocery received a special delivery letter. It contained a hand-written note demanding $5,000 or "you will be killed just like your father." Chester notified the police. As detectives watched from hiding, Chester followed the instructions in the letter. He put the money in a box with a red wrapper and brought it to a downtown restaurant, where he was to receive additional instructions. No one showed up.

IN July Hamilton went on trial in the same courtroom. Aside from a different judge, it was in most respects a replay of Witt's trial. In one important aspect, it wasn't.

Unimpressed by claims of coercion, Judge Fred Hines allowed the prosecution to introduce Hamilton's confession. He did permit Hamilton to take the stand and deny signing the paper. For once, the usually cool Hamilton was visibly upset. "I did not kill Jackson," he yelled. He swore he was in Iola at the time.

Again Stockberger was one of the witnesses. Again Chester Jackson reached the stand. He stared at Hamilton. "That's him," he declared firmly. "You fired at Dad point-blank, and you tried to kill me, too." Spectators were impressed by Chester's cool, methodical testimony. "He was within three feet of me when he fired," Chester told the jury. "He yelled for us to throw out the money. I asked him not to shoot and said I would give him the money. There were several shots fired. I saw the bandit shoot in father's direction."

A murmur rose when Prosecutor Scifres summoned Hamilton's eighteen-year-old sister, Grace. She grudgingly admitted that she had written to a friend in California love letters the prosecution now had. One letter, Scifres emphasized, clearly proved her brother and the Witts had arrived in Iola on May 29, not May 27.

Ira Holmes countered with many of Hamilton's relatives who swore Louis attended the May 27 birthday party. Scifres rebutted with an Iola neighbor who remembered the trio arriving on the 29th.

If Scifres could get a conviction of Witt without his confession, surely he could get a conviction of Hamilton with his. But this jury couldn't agree; two holdouts had their doubts and no one could change their minds. The judge finally dismissed the panel. Scifres pledged to begin a new trial as soon as possible.

The summer simmered by. In November a new jury heard virtually the same evidence. For the third time, Chester Jackson testified. Again, the defendant testified, insisting on his innocence. This time, Scifres's final argument struck a note. "If you love your homes, your family, if you believe in protecting the rights of society, give a warning to the criminals of Indiana and other states who may venture into her borders by bringing in a verdict of guilty and not turning this poisonous reptile loose to add to his killings."

The jury did just that.

At the state prison Hamilton told the warden he was a member of the International Bible Students Association. He joined Witt on Death Row as their appeals moved to the Indiana Supreme Court. Witt's appeal reached the high court first, and was rejected first.

On Nov. 23, 1933, the prison chaplain and several of Witt's relatives visited him for the last time. For his final meal he ordered a chicken dinner, polished off with two cigars. Two minutes after midnight he was escorted to the Hot Squat. Four minutes of high-voltage electricity ended his life. "That was a brave boy, I'll tell you," the chaplain told a reporter afterward.

While Hamilton waited month after month in his cell in Michigan City for a decision on his appeal, Chester Jackson received a surprise telephone call in Indianapolis in July 1934. Detectives told him an itinerant printer named Reeves Brown, arrested on other charges, had admitted sending Chester the $5,000 extortion note two years earlier. The confession was a relief to Chester in several ways. He wouldn't have to testify, for one thing. Brown would plead guilty and get a seven-year sentence.

There was more good news. The state supreme court rejected Hamilton's appeal. His execution was scheduled for September. The Jackson family's three-year ordeal soon would be over.

At 12:05 a.m. on Sept. 28, 1934, Hamilton was taken from his cell. On his final day he had eaten only ice cream while reading the Bible or visiting with his wife and family. Now he was secured to the electric chair, "calm and unprotesting," in the warden's description, to receive two thousand volts of electricity over a period of about five minutes. At 12:12 a.m., the twenty-eight year old convict was declared dead.

2: MADNESS

THE Standard Grocery chain had the perfect person to take the place of its murdered founder. In a way it was as if there had been no change. Everyone agreed Chester Jackson was a younger version of his enterprising father.

L.A. had schooled his son in the business, taught him every secret, inculcated in him the same work habits and work hours, and educated him in the weaknesses of banks and the menaces of the tax men. Indeed, Chester looked much like his father—the same oval face, large ears, bushy eyebrows, thick-rimmed spectacles, and though he was only thirty-seven, chin already sinking into a pouch. He was balding on the crown of his dark hair and combed a strip all the way over to the other side.

Chester had a kind of genius; he knew instinctively where a grocery store might prosper, where a location promised failure. Emulating his father, he often worked until midnight and seldom took a vacation. Like Lafayette, he developed the habit of keeping cash, often large sums, hidden at home. Home was his residence with his wife, the former Edna Mansfield. One main difference between Chester and his father was that the son tended to be more worldly. He had served in the army during World War I, and he maintained membership in the American Legion.

To all appearances a proper businessman, husband and citizen. Except Chester Jackson had a secret.

He had a mistress.

FROM a young age, Marguerite Viola O'Connell—she preferred Marjorie—was a handful.

She was pretty and rebellious. She rebelled mainly against the man married to her mother, for he was not her father.

Marjorie's mother, Clara O'Connell, had lost three of her children to tuberculosis. When her husband died, Clara took a job caring for the widowed mother of a man named Jesse Montgomery, a seed store clerk who was Clara's old boyfriend. Clara became pregnant with Marjorie, but Mr. Montgomery didn't want to marry her. Marjorie was born in 1910. After this Clara took a factory job and met Bob "Pop" O'Connell. When she married O'Connell, he became Marjorie's stepfather.

Years later, a story would be told in the family. On Decoration Day 1920, Clara took her daughter to the cemetery. Pointing to a tall man standing by a line of granite markers, Clara told the child: "You see that man over there? That man is your father. Go over and talk to him." When Marjorie approached the man, he told her, "Go away, little girl."

That was when Marjorie learned she was illegitimate.

Born in Dublin, O'Connell was a devout Catholic who had divorced his first wife before he met Clara. As a result, they couldn't be married in the Catholic Church, a breach that contributed to his drinking. A machinist by trade, he made a home for his family in an industrial neighborhood of Indianapolis but, according to family stories, eventually spent as much time in neighborhood saloons as he did at home.

"He's not my father," Marjorie told a childhood friend. "I don't have a father." She thought Pop favored Roberta, her half-sister. When she reached her teens, Marjorie ridiculed her stepfather behind his back, even calling him an old drunk.

Marjorie was independent and had a temper. She went out when she wanted to go out, usually on dates with her cousin Genevieve. She tolerated schooling, earning good grades when the mood struck her, enjoying more flirtations and games with boys. She was pretty and she knew it. She had straw-colored hair, impertinent brown eyes, a turned-up nose, and a saucy, determined allure.

Three years older than Marjorie, Genevieve worked at the telephone company. She loved music and dancing, and Marjorie fell into step. The boys who took them out usually were older and sometimes had flasks to sip from as they went to lovers' lanes or movie houses or the giant amusement park in Broad Ripple. Always Marjorie wanted her own way. Genevieve took care not to provoke her cousin's prickly temper. Genevieve laughed as she thought about the night at the fashionable athletic club when Marjorie swung a beer bottle at a woman who made a catty remark. If only Pop O'Connell knew....

Years later, Genevieve wondered if Marjorie might have had a form of schizophrenia.

"She was hard to handle, you know. You couldn't discipline her. She wouldn't listen at all. If she decided to go out and stay out all night, she stayed out all night. And Uncle Robert would never, my understanding is that he would never try to discipline her, because she wouldn't listen to him. So it was up to her mother. And she and her mother had some awful battles, too." Time hadn't ameliorated Genevieve's strong judgment: "She was wild. See, she was weird. And very unpredictable." Marjorie's illegitimacy was at the heart of her anger, Genevieve thought. "She should have had psychiatric help, you know, when she was young. But of course, you know, maybe she's more to be pitied than anything."

When Marjorie quit school and took a job downtown, she found her ticket out of the O'Connell household. An earnest, lanky shoe salesman, Millard Kerl was only a year older. Marjorie first set sights on him because she thought he loved Genevieve, but he didn't. At seventeen, Marjorie O'Connell was married. The union lasted one year.

One day, Genevieve saw Millard on the streetcar. "She was just too much for me," he confessed. "I couldn't handle her at all."

AT the age of eighteen she was Marjorie O'Connell again, single and pretty much broke but hardly without assets. Possessing youth, determination and confidence, she also had good looks, especially good looks. Men turned their heads and stared. Blonde, five feet two and shapely, she knew how to select dresses and makeup to attract the handsomest men with the boldest thoughts.

She worked as a manicurist, then took a job as a clerk at the Murphy's five and dime in downtown Indianapolis. On the day in 1932 when Chester Jackson came in and flirted with her, no one could mistake him for a movie star. Even so, he radiated charm and confidence, the manner of a man accustomed to having his own way. Plain as he could look in his business suits and stiff white shirts, he had a wink of mischief about him, a sense of humor Marjorie found appealing. That Chester was thirty-eight, seventeen years her senior, wasn't especially important. Marjorie preferred older men, and Chester obviously had money, plenty of money.

Chester could entertain Marjorie on a scale she found she liked, and the frequency of their dates increased. That he had been married ten years made no significant difference. His wife, he said, slept with other men. In fact Edna had become pregnant by another man and delivered a daughter in 1929. Eventually, Chester arranged for Marjorie to live in a fancy downtown hotel. Later, after Edna moved out, Marjorie moved into Chester's old residence on the far north side of the city.

In 1933 Chester wrote to his attorney:

> I have given you specific instructions about writing my will in which I have not directed any provision whatever to be made for the young daughter of Edna Jackson, my wife, for the reason that she is not my child. I have never seen the child and did not have intercourse with my wife for at least two years and in fact much longer than that before the child was borne. I know that I am not the father of this child.

They were comfortable this way, as lovers rather than husband and wife. Calling Marjorie his million dollar baby from the five and ten cent store, Chester gave her everything she wanted. What the prominent people of Indianapolis whispered in their clubs and parlors didn't matter so long as the appearance of propriety was maintained, and they were good at appearances. With her at his side, Chester seemed younger.

In their first years she tolerated his long absences at work and soothed him when the trauma of the Witt and Hamilton trials and the extortion attempt left him shaking. When he left to scout out a new store location or pursue other business interests—the family had stock in Illinois coal properties—she begrudged his absences and chided him upon his return. She could be a demanding, scolding mistress. To fill the time, she began practicing on the piano and decided she had talent. Chester promised her the best lessons available. Later, Marjorie told neighbors she had training at the famous Julliard School in New York.

Only occasionally did she return home. The O'Connells had left their old home for a newer residence on the east side of the city. When Marjorie visited her mother she demonstrated that her temper had hardly mellowed; she made pointed comments about her illegitimacy. On such visits Pop O'Connell acted politely. Before Pop died, Marjorie knew he had visited a priest to discuss re-entering the Catholic Church.

At least Chester's family seemed more settled and amiable. His younger brother Howard, though not always in the best of health, worked beside Chester in the grocery business. Sister Charlotte was a strong, independent woman who wouldn't marry until late in life. Only Marguerite, the only child of L.A.'s second marriage, was apart. After their father's murder, the brothers claimed, Marguerite had demanded too much for her interest in the estate. Bitter feelings preceded Marguerite's divorce from Ed Wiest and her move to California to forge her own independent future.

Just before the beginning of World War II, Chester and Marjorie moved to Woodruff Place, a four-square block enclave carved into the near east side of Indianapolis. The neighborhood featured spacious homes with mansard roofs and colonnaded porches. It had broad, esplanaded streets lined with majestic trees, ornate fountains and statues. Their home was a large gold and cream house. The downstairs rooms had high ceilings with fancy chandeliers. Upstairs were four bedrooms. Marjorie finally had all the material things she had so little of as a child. She drove a new Cadillac. Chester bought her furs and jewelry, including a necklace with fifty-five diamonds.

For a time Clara O'Connell moved in with them. Marjorie's widowed mother read palms to bring in extra money for herself. Mother and daughter maintained a fragile co-existence. While the neighbors thought Chester and Marjorie were husband and wife, Clara knew better. To neighborhood acquaintances, Marjorie was a pleasant conversationalist who played bridge skillfully, worked long hours in her yard, and played the piano. These glimpses masked Marjorie's growing bitterness. Increasingly she resented Chester's absences. Increasingly she quarreled with her mother. When Clara finally moved out, she was relieved to get away from the acrimony.

When Chester came home at night he would wait in the alley until Marjorie turned on the garage light. Inside, she complained of his long hours, of being alone. When he bought her two husky chow dogs for protection, she found something else to criticize. She wanted to travel and have fun while she was still young while Chester had to work, work, work. As the war dragged on, she was given to sharper changes in mood, more unpredictability. She became more possessive and more jealous. If Chester ever left her, she warned, she would kill herself and maybe him, too.

To friends and family members who had glimpses of these changes, Chester was being worn down. He gave in, as he had to give in. In 1947, on the fiftieth anniversary of the opening of L.A.'s first store, he sold all of his interests in Standard Grocery to the A&P chain. Chester was fifty-four.

The sale meant millions of dollars, of course. No one knew how much money Chester really had. For years it had been his practice to occasionally bring home cash from the business. This he kept hidden in closets and other places. He had a morbid fear of the Internal Revenue Service. Now he had a new will written and designated $300,000 for Marjorie, identifying her as the woman "with whom I have lived these many years."

He didn't tell Marjorie he had quietly divorced Edna three years earlier.

ONE June afternoon in 1952, everything in Marjorie O'Connell's life changed.

She had lunch with a friend. During casual conversation, the friend mentioned hearing that Chester had divorced Edna in 1945. This was how Marjorie discovered that the man with whom she had lived for more than two decades had betrayed her with his silence for seven years.

No one would ever know the emotions she experienced, but surely they included disgust and humiliation. The confrontation that followed must have been volcanic.

Chester arranged with his lawyers so they could fill out the marriage forms in private. Thus none of the snoopy clerks at the Marion County Courthouse could smugly note the differences between them. He looked older than his fifty-eight years; she looked younger than her forty-one. On his application Chester mistakenly wrote "Marguerite Jackson" as the woman he planned to marry, scratched the surname, and added O'Connell. To the question of whether this was her first marriage, Marjorie wrote yes. In a sense, perhaps, it was. So, with the private July ceremony, their marriage began with a small lie.

No piece of paper could change their relationship. It had changed in subtle ways over the years. Nearly bald and somewhat stooped, Chester had lost his youthful gait. Marjorie had her energy and her temper, and she dominated the relationship. They were wealthy people, and she wanted to use their wealth. She drove to Chicago and spent thousands of dollars on new shoes and more jewelry. She bought a new Cadillac, a smarter design than the old one. She took French lessons. And she insisted on traveling, to New York, Arizona, Las Vegas, Cuba.

Whatever she wanted she got. Such protests as Chester made, and they were few, came meekly.

They maintained separate bedrooms.

In the eyes of old friends, the retired grocery executive changed rapidly, troubled by his idleness and the increasingly dominant role of his wife. He liked to read the Wall Street Journal and Sports Illustrated but could not always concentrate. Chester's mood darkened in another way. He began talking about threats from years ago from the two men who had murdered his father. He began to watch the street outside his home. Any strangers worried him. At night he peered anxiously through a crack in the curtains.

Robbers had killed his father and now, more and more, he dreamed of his own murder. He bought a silver revolver to keep by his bedside. One night, Chester seized the gun and, wearing only pajamas, ran out into the street. "They're going to get me!" he screamed. "They're going to get me!"

After her husband was safely in the hospital Marjorie asked the doctors how long these spells might last. They described a combination of things: the loss of his business life had weighed heavily on Chester; the phantasm of murder had lingered too long, and Chester also worried about the health of his invalid brother Howard and the recent death of his ex-brother-in-law. Rest, care and time would help. Nevertheless, one doctor predicted, Chester would have a recurrence within five years.

Marjorie turned to Don Screes for help.

It was Screes who had taken away the revolver, helped Chester to calm down, quieted the demons. A short, friendly man with an easy-going demeanor,

Screes had spent most of his career working for Chester and Standard Grocery, and regarded his former boss as a second father. Now Screes made the arrangements to get Chester under the care of the best psychiatrists in the country, in Baltimore.

Marjorie wouldn't have to worry about her husband's business investments or bills. Chester gave Screes power of attorney to manage his finances.

Two months of treatment in Maryland worked wonders. Chester telephoned Screes long-distance. "We're going to Florida," he announced, sounding like his old self. "I'll let you know when we get there." He instructed his friend to wire $4,000 in traveler's checks. When they returned to Indianapolis several weeks later, Screes remembered, "He seemed fine. She was as shrewish and unpredictable as ever."

Chester was well enough to go house-hunting. More than anything, Marjorie wanted a place with privacy. Not just a house to call home, but one with special things to set it apart from other people. For several weeks they examined homes in Meridian Hills, a prosperous northern section of Indianapolis which had its own police patrols. Chester's now widowed sister Charlotte had lived in the area since the 1930s.

On scenic Spring Mill Drive they found their house. The seven-room ranch-style residence was comfortable though not ornate. Such a house could be found in any neighborhood of young doctors and businessmen still called junior as well as executive. It paled compared to some of the stately mansions farther down Spring Mill on the other side of the street, on bluffs overlooking the White River. Yet the property had a large lot thick with trees and bushes. There would be no neighbors to the north, because of a cross street, nor to the east, across Spring Mill, because of the Meridian Hills Country Club, itself screened by trees and bushes. They bought the house in 1954, for $100,850 cash.

Over the next few years they secured their privacy to the west, purchasing two adjoining lots for a total of $17,500. Marjorie arranged for a chest-high wire fence. At the front driveway the two separate gates could be secured by padlocks. The driveway was almost a circle, but on the south side it extended past the house and turned behind, so cars could be parked in any of the four bays out of sight of nosy eyes. Paving stones led to a door next to the Florida room at the rear, and again to a gate in the fence on 65th Street.

After they settled in Marjorie wanted to travel again. In 1957 Chester took her around the world, their last major trip. Marjorie seemed strangely affected by the experience, especially by their visit to a Moslem mosque and orphanage. Only a few short trips to Florida or New York came after that.

One reason was Chester's continuing debilitation. At times he required the care of a private nurse. For several months he had to be hospitalized again. Around the house he seemed feebler, unable to enjoy old interests like the Masonic memberships he had maintained since the 1930s. Material things meant little. He had a hundred and fifty pairs of shoes, few places to wear them.

Money was no problem. For years Chester never allowed the balance of his checking account to drop below $1,000,000. They owned three Cadillacs. Money poured in. From 1957 through 1962 Chester collected nearly $684,000 from one coal investment, and had the funds deposited in his non-interest checking account. Yet each year he directed Screes to donate $2 to a Protestant orphanage.

Screes kept his peace when he visited the house on Spring Mill. For all of his affection for Chester, Screes disliked Marjorie. He felt sorry for his old boss. Any fire Chester once had now seemed permanently snuffed out. Visiting the house could be an adventure; Screes never knew when Marjorie would start one of her verbal tantrums. Always Chester gave in.

One day, Screes ran into his aging friend at the neighborhood market. Chester looked weak and nervous, obviously upset over some new altercation.

"Chester," Screes asked bluntly, "why in hell don't you get rid of her?"

"I can't," Chester answered. "She's such a good cook and a good housekeeper."

On another occasion Chester and Screes were sitting in the garage talking about old times when Marjorie roared up in her Cadillac and dented the wall as she screeched to a halt.

Chester just shook his head.

EVER since her visit to the Holy Land on their world tour, Marjorie had become transfixed at how faith in a higher being uplifted the people over the grimness of poverty and circumstances. When the couple returned home she began to read the Bible regularly, plunging into the book like someone pulled into a dream. Hour after hour she sought the revelations of Scripture. She memorized passages and nodded as some line or verse revealed an epiphany.

These things Don Screes learned little by little.

Although she claimed to be a Catholic, Marjorie did not attend church regularly. If she had been searching for answers all of her life, Screes thought, she certainly believed now she knew where to find them. Not that it did Chester much good. His depression recurred, and with it the hallucinations. Screes helped to arrange extended care in a Louisville hospital. Shock treatments were provided, over Marjorie's objections. Screes held his tongue. In truth he thought she needed psychiatric attention as much as his old boss and friend. They had lost most of their few friends, and doted on their pet parrot, Boy.

How eccentric were they? Screes always would remember that day in the 1950s when Chester telephoned. The voice didn't sound quite as certain as it used to, but Chester asked Screes to stop by the house for a special errand. Chester wanted him to pick up some parcels, then drive downtown to meet his nephew and brother-in-law to transport some cash from a safety deposit box to the house on Spring Mill.

A messenger's job, the kind Screes had been doing for years.

When he arrived, Marjorie, friendly enough, let him in and asked him to wait. A house of organized comfort, Screes thought, a house reflecting more of the matron's taste than her husband's. Heavy pink drapes, blue walls, the turquoise carpet in the living room, luxurious throw rugs trailing off into the other rooms. A Chinese short-top desk held several delicate Swiss music boxes. A marble-top table supported a birdcage lamp. And the piano, of course, the baby grand, Marjorie's pride and joy.

Marjorie gave Screes two shopping bags and a shoebox. Then he drove downtown as instructed. The safety deposit box was in the Indiana Trust Co. There Screes met Ed Wiest and Chester's brother-in-law, Ray Koers, a city policeman who was married to Marjorie's half-sister, Roberta. Marjorie didn't like Ray, apparently because he became a cop instead of a priest. Screes never told her that Chester occasionally gave Ray money to support his growing family.

From the security box they transferred thick packets of money, bundles of old money, into the bags and shoebox. Some of it was wrapped, but Screes saw numerous loose $100 and $20 bills. Although the three men said little, Screes was dumbfounded. There must be $2,000,000 in cash, maybe more, he thought.

He wondered how much cash Chester had squirreled away over the years.

Screes and the policeman took the money to the house on Spring Mill. Chester carried the parcels into the bedroom. Somehow, Screes knew the cash would remain there.

SIGNED by Chester's attorney, the letter was dated Aug. 12, 1964, and titled *Re: Accounting as to Power of Attorney of Chester Jackson.* The three pieces of paper sought to repudiate twelve years of trust in twelve paragraphs of poisonous implications and allegations.

Screes read the letter carefully.

Mr. Jackson has received the accounting which you supplied him for the period 1952 to 1964, during which period of time you exercised certain rights under the power of attorney granted to you by him...At present there are several transactions indicated which Mr. Jackson is questioning at this time since he either has no recollection at this time for granting such authority or is unable to satisfy himself at present to such transactions without a full explanation.

It went on and on. A $40,000 loan Chester had approved for Screes but could not remember. Various times he gave Marjorie cash, which she no longer could remember. Dozens of expenditures, cash and checks, for cars, gifts, and other expenses, like $485 to Ray Koers.

More letters came.

I have just received a call from Mr. Jackson whereby he has requested that he be furnished the complete list or record of any and all transactions, business or otherwise, which you handled for him during the period of time from October 15, 1963, through March 10, 1964. It appears Mr. Jackson was in the hospital most of the time, and as a result does not have a recollection or record of what took place during this period.

And:

Mr. Jackson has called to my attention the fact that he has had several safety deposit boxes at various banks. He has further advised me that while you exercised the powers under the power of attorney which you previously had for Mr. Jackson, you had control over these various safety deposit boxes. Mr. Jackson is now requesting that he be supplied with the names and locations of each safety deposit box under his name during the period of time that the power of attorney was enforced.

Thirty years of service to the Jackson family and it came down to this. Well, Screes thought, whatever the attorney had to say, crazy Marjorie really would be doing the talking.

Jews were her newest obsession. She told Screes and a few friends that the Jews had killed Christ and were evil. She talked compulsively about the Bible and the flood of revelations it bestowed in her. She had turned on Screes with a vengeance. Screes had put her husband in a Baltimore nuthouse and plotted to steal their money, she decided. Not only Screes but everyone took advantage of them due to Chester's infirmities. And it wasn't just a few thousand dollars they wanted, or a few hundred thousand; they wanted all the money.

Sitting in the living room with her weakened husband day after day, Marjorie constructed a scenario in which Screes wanted to steal the Southwest Illinois Coal Corp. from them.

The facts were simple enough. In the 1930s the Jackson family had acquired vast amounts of coal-rich Illinois land at small cost. Eventually they held 3,000 shares of stock in the company, nearly seventy-five percent, collected in a single certificate. Company records showed this certificate had been divided into three certificates of 1,000 shares each in 1952. One was for Chester, one for brother Howard, and one for their sister, Charlotte. At the time Chester held the nominal title of company president, but Don Screes, an assistant officer, really watched his interests.

Howard and Charlotte had designated their stock to their nephew and niece, the children of their half-sister, Marguerite. Although Chester also had once made the same designation, he had since revoked the bequest in favor of Marjorie. Upon Charlotte's recent death, Marguerite's children were to receive not only the bulk of her estate, more than $1,000,000, but her coal stock as well. They would benefit similarly when Howard died. Only recently Howard had changed his will so Chester no longer would be executor.

To Marjorie all of this was nothing more than a well-conceived plot to deprive Chester and Marjorie Jackson of what was rightfully theirs. Marguerite's

children had a third of the stock, stood to own two
thirds, and probably had a scheme cooking to get
Chester's. On New Year's Day 1965, when the phone
rang with the news of Howard's death, Marjorie
decided they would have to go to court.

Chester's lawyers filed two lawsuits. One
contested codicils to Howard's will; the other, against
Southwest Illinois Coal, contended the 1952 stock
division had been arranged through forgery and
without Chester's knowledge.

Screes fought back.

In the matter of the power of attorney over
Chester's finances, he could provide a meticulously
detailed list of expenditures over twelve years. On the
coal stock, he wondered, and argued, how Chester
could now challenge the stock division when it had
been Chester's own idea? How could Chester claim
fraudulent division and explain the silence of his own
brother and sister in the years since? In fact how
could Chester challenge the stock when for more than
a decade he had voted only his own 1,000 shares
without protest?

Screes thought of the hundreds of hours he
had sat in Chester's home watching his old friend
change. He loved the man. He believed—always
would believe—that Chester was a great man. And
now their friendship ended.

In the house on Spring Mill, a kind of shared
madness reigned. Increasingly feeble, Chester was
largely dependent on the whims of his increasingly
paranoid wife. Both doted on their parrot; an oil

portrait of Boy graced the living room wall, and one Christmas Marjorie bought Boy a doll. The bird could say both of their names.

Now, when Boy died, Marjorie and Chester were grief-stricken. Carrying Boy in a cloth, Marjorie went to a neighbor for help. With the neighbor's assistance they buried the pet in the yard. With tears in her eyes and a rosary knotted in her hand, Marjorie prayed for Boy. Not long after this, in 1969, her mother, eighty-six and feeble, passed away.

The Jacksons had few visitors. Marjorie read her Bibles and played the piano. She learned to play the accordion and picked at a five-string guitar. When she went out she wore a disguise. She put on fur hats and fur coats and made herself look beautiful—or normal, like one of them.

As the months passed, Chester spent more time in bed. When the lawyers telephoned to announce their setbacks or defeats in court, this only confirmed what Marjorie expected anyway: the attorneys and judges were all of a cloth, cheaters and plotters.

The lawsuit against Howard's estate failed. The appeal failed. Four additional legal maneuvers were dismissed. Only the lawsuit against the coal company remained, and the lawyers were not optimistic. And Don Screes filed a countersuit, charging that he was the target of reckless litigation.

On Oct. 18, 1970, all of this ended for Chester. He died of an embolism, age seventy-seven.

Marjorie did not go to Chester's funeral. For now everything had come full circle. Marjorie believed her husband of eighteen years, her companion of thirty-nine years, was a Jew.

3: THE BANKER

To all appearances, Herbert Dale Biddle, Jr., was the perfect son, the perfect husband, the perfect father, and, most important of all, the perfect banker. He was completely trustworthy. In fact, he was so trustworthy he became a vice-president and Trust Officer in the Trust Division of Indiana National Bank, the state's second-largest financial institution.

Everyone who knew Herb Biddle liked him as well; he was an up-and-comer, the kind of polite young man you wished your daughter had met. As he entered his early thirties, Herb was a former Marine, a graduate of Butler University, a graduate of the Indiana University School of Law, and a man who had moved steadily upward since joining Indiana National Bank as a trainee in 1964. So smart and reliable was he that in just six short years the bank gave him responsibility for the Trust Division section administering estate and guardianship accounts.

Herb was a joiner. He served on bar association committees and as a delegate to the state bar's annual convention. He had been president of the Central Indiana Corporate Fiduciaries Association. He was president of Butler University's B-Men's Association for former athletes and then president of the Butler Alumni Association.

The list went on. He was a guest lecturer, a member of the right clubs. He was a devout Christian Scientist. He was married to a pretty woman gifted as a teacher and choreographer. They had a son and daughter.

At Christmas time Herb played neighborhood Santa.

Upon the death of Chester Jackson, Biddle took over the management of his estate and bank accounts.

MARJORIE Jackson slammed down the phone. She had lost count of the number of times she had sternly informed her caller not to bother her. She had absolutely no intention of going downtown to listen to their lies and sweet seductions, absolutely no intention of allowing Mr. Biddle, from the bank, or anyone else to enter her home for the purpose of signing papers or anything else.

Since Chester's death she had steadfastly retreated from the things she thought were poisoned with sin and greed. From sundown Tuesdays until dusk on Sundays she studied the Bible and prayed. This ritual allowed no variation, for these were times of revelation. She sensed a seven-year cycle of death; Chester's passing marked the beginning of this passage. What lay at the end? Those things which would grow would grow; those God wanted to die, would die. All else was mystery.

The house was her sanctuary. Here she had everything anyone could need: at least several million dollars, crammed in shoeboxes and other hiding places; her Bibles, her privacy, her organ, her three pianos. She could play a Chopin waltz or *My Gal Sal* or *Hawaiian Hospitality*.

Needing little of the world, she gradually shut the world out. She regarded her property as part of herself and trespass as a violation as repulsive as rape. Lights burned day and night, magic candles to ward off intruders. Padlocks secured the two gates at the driveway and the fence gate on the north side. The NO TRESPASSING sign in front seemed emphatic, even more ominous as the bushes and weeds grew in wild riot. Looking at the place, no one could get a sense of welcome. Keep away. Stay out.

Marjorie knew she was rejecting all of the things she could command in the world of people. Certainly with her wealth she could have anything she wanted. She might be the toast of the city, a rich widow in her mature years. She looked ten years younger than her sixty-one years, and she took care of herself, having her hair fixed professionally each week, using makeup and wearing attractive dresses.

But, she realized, if *they* knew that *she* knew, they would try to destroy her. So she had to play-act.

Occasionally she lunched with acquaintances from the old days. At such times she gave only careful glimpses of her meditations, her opinions, her fears

and obsessions. She was a brilliant liar, playing the
role of the chatty woman, talking of her piano playing,
some new dress, the problems of the world, Vietnam,
yes, and Nixon. How distressing the affairs of man.

Actually she ventured out reluctantly and with
purpose. Usually she left the house only in early week,
before Tuesday dusk. She went shopping, buying
things on whim, yet also stocking up for the eventual
cataclysm and for a special visit, from Jesus. She
bought dozens of pairs of shoes and gradually
accumulated fifty sets of pajamas. If something went
wrong with one thing, she would have another
without having to go out to buy the item.

Each week she purchased fresh-cut flowers.
Also she went to the specialty shop in the nearest
shopping plaza to fill a bag with the richest cheeses.
She bought several hundred jars of peanut butter,
honey and vegetables. To the sales clerks she offered
good humor, paid for her purchases with large and
sometimes old bills, and seemed not at all worried
about the change.

She drove directly home, unlocked the front
gate, pulled her Cadillac inside, locked the gate, and
parked the car in the garage. Alone inside, she
watched TV, read how-to books on health, and played
the piano. She began leaving out cookies, cakes, and
pies for Jesus to eat. In the realization that demons
and devils could enter the house, she carefully
wrapped aluminum foil over most of the windows
and put foil on the doorknobs and air ducts.

If the house now felt protected, by extension the yard had to be similarly readied. The fence circumscribed her world, a sanctuary of slightly more than three and a half acres. Here, she decided, things must grow as God wanted. So as the maples and birches grew, as the weeds flourished and interlocked, what had been a lawn disappeared under the advances of unspoiled growth. Her neighbors complained, first to her, then to the authorities. Not only were weeds as high as three feet, not only had the grass disappeared into an ugly swale, with weeds sprouting from cracks in the driveway, Mrs. Jackson collected her trash in green plastic bags and threw them over the fence, there to wait days for the collection trucks. The yard looked like a jungle.

Marjorie spent hours patrolling her property. The birds and squirrels and butterflies were her friends. In one room inside she kept dozens of bags of popcorn. Sometimes, she revealed to a neighbor, she could hear the little creatures talking to her in squeaky voices. As often she would launch into a lecture mixing ecology and theology.

The Board of Health sent postcard warnings; she threw them in the wastebasket.

To the marshals and deputies who stopped occasionally on 65th Street to inquire of her welfare, Marjorie unleashed stories of violated privacy. She thought police officers could be tolerated, and she could confide in them her complaints. Someone had tossed a foundation stone through a window; kids jumped the fence and ran through her yard with wanton recklessness. Once in awhile children taunted her from a distance, knowing she was a widow without the means to retaliate.

She did not dislike all of the children. She allowed one neighbor boy to mow the right-of-way outside the fence and paid him with two $20 bills, one of them a rare Philadelphia Reserve note worth eight times the face amount.

CHESTER'S final will was short and simple.

Written on April 20, 1970, and witnessed by his attorneys, the document only had three provisions. One was for the payment of just debts; another for having Indiana National Bank and Marjorie as personal representatives of his estate. The other was the most important: "I hereby give, bequeath and devise any and all property that I may have at the time of my death, including real, personal and mixed, to my beloved wife, Marjorie V. Jackson."

There was just one problem. Marjorie.

Mrs. Jackson told the attorneys she would have nothing to do with any estate proceedings. Under no circumstances would she sign anything. She told Biddle the same thing. Nor would she allow anyone to visit her home.

The judge in Marion County Probate Court wasn't happy. It looked like the estate would weigh in at more than $7,000,000, not including the disputed Illinois coal property, and a woman claiming to be

Chester's daughter from his first marriage filed a petition of heirship. That could be settled with blood tests. In any event, the judge knew the widow would have to sign something. There could be no settlement without her signature.

Marjorie was adamant. When one of the attorneys called to suggest the possibility of settling all of the litigation over Southwest Illinois Coal Corp., she hung up.

Reluctantly, the judge did the only thing he could think of. He issued a subpoena ordering Marjorie to appear in court on March 9, 1971, or face arrest for contempt of court.

Just one city block from the downtown site where L.A. Jackson opened his first grocery store, the City-County Building now towered twenty-eight stories. Probate Court occupied a considerable section of the fifteenth floor. It was a strange, and brief, hearing. The widow, beautifully dressed and smiling, appeared to pay little attention. The lawyers discussed the need to settle the coal land litigation, since all the other parties were willing, and to invest the Jackson estate by some reasonable means, perhaps an agency agreement by which the bank would select the investments and Mrs. Jackson wouldn't have to worry about the details.

Finally, the judge spoke to Marjorie. She answered his questions carefully and patiently. "Whatever you do is fine with me," she said. "I'll leave it up to the court to do as they please."

Jim Stewart, one of her attorneys, telephoned Marjorie the next day. As a result of the hearing, they were considering means to reach a settlement so the coal company could be sold. Would she be willing to authorize someone to execute the necessary papers?

Stewart's memo of the conversation crystallized Marjorie's mental state and attitude.

Mrs. Jackson immediately bristled and said under no circumstances was she going to authorize anybody to do anything, that she considered the matter to be in the hands of the court and that the court had all the authority necessary. I tried to explain that we still needed someone to sign the settlement documents. She then suggested that the court sign, but when I asked her if she was willing to authorize the court in writing to sign for her or appoint someone to sign for her, her answer was an emphatic "no." She mentioned that she felt that she was treated like dirt or garbage in the courtroom by everyone; that a pack of lies and nothing new had been told; that everyone sided against her and were all out to get her money; that she didn't want to talk to any lawyers or anyone else further about the subject; she emphasized that she was not coming back into court again.

Stewart asked if she had any family, friends or any minister or church member she could talk to or authorize to act in her behalf.

She said no, she couldn't trust any of her family, that she had no friends, that she went to church in her own home, and that there was no one she would be willing to authorize in writing to do anything for her.

Ultimately, the judge had no recourse.

As Biddle explained the situation to Marjorie over the phone, the court had appointed an Indianapolis attorney and former state supreme court justice to act as her temporary guardian. In her behalf, then, he signed all the necessary papers to wrap up the Southwest Illinois Coal Co. question, settle all of the old litigation, and prepare for the sale of the stock.

Biddle sent neatly worded letters and made polite telephone calls. While maintaining a pile of correspondence, Marjorie refused to reply. She realized Chester's nephew and niece would benefit handsomely from the sale of the company because, as Biddle noted, the value of the land had skyrocketed due to a national energy emergency. Still, even Biddle seemed impressed by the outcome. More than $12,000,000 would be funneled into Chester's estate.

Marjorie would get most of the money; the woman who claimed to be Chester's daughter had accepted a nuisance settlement of $60,000. As things followed their normal course, as bills and taxes were paid, Biddle planned to transfer more than $7,000,000 into Marjorie's personal account at the bank, making the aggregate well over $8,000,000.

Naturally, Biddle thought this should earn interest. By signing an agency account, he suggested, the bank could judiciously invest her funds.

Marjorie finally decided to stop answering the telephone. As months went by she read and threw away numerous letters from her attorneys and banker imploring her to cooperate with them.

One afternoon, as Marjorie worked in her yard, she noticed Biddle talking to her neighbors. She ran into the house. When the phone rang a few minutes later, she didn't answer. In a few days a registered letter arrived. "As I informed you previously by letter," Biddle wrote, "a substantial amount of money is available for distribution to you." He wanted to meet with her personally. He would be outside her gate at nine o'clock the next morning.

She refused to come out of the house.

On June 22, 1973, a letter arrived from the judge. "Your refusal to communicate with the bank or attorneys is quite disturbing and I am wondering if I cannot be of some assistance to you under the circumstances. I am again requesting that you contact me."

Matters might have remained at a frustrating stalemate had a sheriff's deputy not appeared at Marjorie's door in August. He informed her she was under arrest for failure to heed a Board of Health citation and earlier warnings to clean up her property. She would have to submit to fingerprinting like a common criminal, and pay a fine.

It was a turning point whose impact could only be speculated.

Probably Marjorie saw it as a sign from God telling her that sooner or later she would have to deal with these people. In any event, she began answering Biddle's phone calls. She consented to an agency arrangement giving the bank authorization to invest her millions. She would even allow some modest gardening around her house. She signed the agreement on Dec. 10, 1973.

A few days later, Biddle wrote to her attorneys saying he wanted to assign part of the assets of her estate to the investment account before the end of the year. Among other things, he wrote:

> I would hope that our relationship with her can mature in the coming months so that we would be in a position to suggest to her that she do some additional estate planning, perhaps to the extent of executing a Will and/or an inter vivos trust....I am of the opinion that she has the ability to know the objects of her bounty. She appears simply to be an eccentric person who desires to be left alone and to enjoy her music and her religious beliefs.

Month after month into 1974 and then 1975, Marjorie read Biddle's accountings as the mailman delivered them over the fence. Undoubtedly the young banker misinterpreted her lack of cooperation as a combination of apathy and ignorance. In the long years of acrimonious litigation, Marjorie learned how to read financial numbers, and as Don Screes observed in another context, "She had a memory like an elephant."

One thing that troubled the woman now were Biddle's notations about buying school bonds. She knew nothing about such bonds.

Marjorie liked the pretty young receptionist at her dentist's office. The girl always made it a point to be friendly. On one visit to have her teeth cleaned, Mrs. Jackson confided a secret: Her banker was robbing her. But she didn't have to worry, she said, because a man from Chicago had agreed to build a secret safe in her home. By paying him extra she knew he never would reveal the location. No one from the bank would be able to find the safe.

The receptionist listened with fascination. Mrs. Jackson was one of their most interesting patients.

Exactly when Marjorie found out about Biddle's career change isn't known. Announcing plans to join a local law firm, Biddle's departure from Indiana National Bank was effective as of Dec. 31, 1975. Nine days later, Marjorie drove downtown to the thirty-eight story bank tower and demanded and received $500,000 cash from her account. Guards brought out the money in thick bundles which were transferred to the trunk of her Cadillac in the turn-around under the garage at the rear of the bank.

The withdrawal sent ripples of alarm all the way to the Trust Division. Three days later, a senior bank officer telephoned Marjorie. As a matter of routine, he explained, Mr. Biddle's investment practices were being reviewed. Could Mrs. Jackson provide information about more than $600,000 in bonds which seemed to have been misplaced?

Mrs. Jackson could not.

The next day Marjorie returned downtown and demanded $500,000 cash. The next week, she collected a total of $1,000,000 cash. One week later, she showed up again.

This time the bank officer turned her down.

"I'm sorry, Mrs. Jackson," he explained. "Your account has been frozen by court order."

THE secretary flashed a signal while Marjorie waited. Moments later the judge came out of his office, extending his hand. Before he reached the reception area, Marjorie flared at him: "What right do you have to tie up my bank account?"

Judge Victor Pfau gulped.

He expected an elderly, senile, perhaps ragtag woman. The lady standing here now looked like nothing so much as an angry society matron ready to dress down an inefficient caterer. Marjorie Jackson's platinum hair had been fashioned chicly. Though wrinkled, her skin showed signs of attentive makeup. Short, perhaps five-two, with demanding brown eyes, a high forehead and pronounced cheek structure, she seemed independent and sure of herself. The clothes looked expensive.

"Well, I'm concerned about your welfare," Pfau said as he guided her into his chambers.

"What do you care about my money?" Marjorie bristled. "If I didn't have it and someone knocked me on the head, you wouldn't care then."

Pfau was an affable man who had an uncanny resemblance to actor Peter Sellers in one of his character roles. In one of his campaigns the signs urged "Vote for Judge Pfau. The P is silent. The rest rhymes with cow." Within his domain, however, he yielded considerable power, presiding over thousands of estates and trusts and the lucrative appointments and fees that went with them.

The judge studied his surprise visitor. When the Indiana National Bank officer had called, he described an eccentric widow who, to the bank's shock, had withdrawn $2,000,000 from her account. To accommodate her, the bank had to order new bills from the Federal Reserve Bank in Chicago. Mrs. Jackson then hauled the cash away in grocery sacks.

Naturally, Pfau's first thought went to the possibility of swindle. Older persons made inviting prey. The old court files on the estate of Chester Jackson suggested numerous problems with his widow, including the appointment of a temporary guardian. Perhaps at sixty-five Mrs. Jackson was fading mentally. It didn't make sense for someone to withdraw millions in cash. So, without formal hearing, Pfau had signed a temporary restraining order.

In person Marjorie showed not the slightest sign of being out of touch with reality. As if she could read his thoughts, she announced she could speak several languages, she understood the nature of money, and she simply didn't trust the bank to administer her funds any longer, as was her right.

But, the judge cautioned, keeping such large sums in her home was hardly wise.

Marjorie held up a handful of keys. "You don't think I'm stupid, do you?"

"Mrs. Jackson, if you put it in safety deposit boxes you'll lose the interest."

Marjorie laughed. "Who wants interest? I have more money than I'll ever spend, and I'd just have to pay taxes on interest."

"But, cash....why don't you get certified checks? It's much safer."

"Why should I be afraid? I've got three separate burglar alarms. My husband told me to keep large amounts of money on hand so I'll have it if I need it. My husband told me how to handle money, and he had more money than you'll ever see."

Pfau slowly lit a cigar. Trying to be diplomatic, he commented on her attractive dress.

"I bought this at J.C. Penney's for nineteen dollars," Marjorie said pointedly.

"I understand you let your grass grow...."

Marjorie launched into a lecture on ecology. The city would become a Sodom and Gomorrah with all of the spreading concrete and the way people poured chemical poisons on beautiful, natural things. "My yard is just the way God intended. I wake up in the morning and I see birds and butterflies."

All very well, Pfau conceded. But perhaps she needed someone to protect her interests. "I've got to protect you whether you want me to or not."

Marjorie shook her head. "God protects me."

Well, the judge pressed, perhaps she should retain an attorney.

Marjorie reddened. "Attorney? Why do I need an attorney?" Not only did she not trust lawyers, she simply had no need for them. Nor did she trust her few relatives.

Pfau suggested her family physician for counsel.

"My physician walks with me all the time," Marjorie said.

His suggestions exhausted, Pfau decided to give the matter further thought. In fact he would delay any hearing on the restraining order for one week. For the moment this was all he would promise.

Marjorie left the office and took the elevator to the main floor. When she got outside, she blew a kiss to the sun.

AFTER the meeting, Pfau arranged for the Marion County Prosecutor's Office to keep a watch on the woman. Investigators kept the house under surveillance and followed Marjorie when she went out. They noticed nothing out of the ordinary. No one visited the house. There were no indications of strange phone calls.

In court a week later, Feb. 9, 1976, Marjorie took the witness stand.

"I have not signed anything and I'm not about to," she said firmly. "That's how my husband got into trouble, signing some papers. My husband told me never to sign anything."

Pfau listened carefully. She had an answer for everything. He could not and would not declare her sufficiently incompetent to have a guardian. She was peculiar, not incompetent, and the law did not prohibit peculiarity. He decided to rescind his order but to make the decision effective in another eight days. This would give the prosecutor's staff additional time to observe her.

In fact, a sheriff's sergeant was posted near her home, and two investigators from the prosecutor's office followed as Marjorie left the court and retrieved her white Cadillac from the no-parking zone where she had left it. She drove to the north side of the city, into the Broad Ripple area. She bought eight bags of groceries at an A&P, purchased two wheelbarrows at a hardware store, and collected two bags of articles at a drugstore. She drove four miles to another shopping plaza, went into a supermarket and purchased six more bags of groceries. Then she drove about a mile to another A&P and filled four more bags with groceries, including a half-dozen loaves of bread and two dozen boxes of powdered-sugar doughnuts. She went back to Broad Ripple and bought flowers.

She spent a total of five hours shopping before she went home.

In their surveillance report, investigators Becky Wanick and Dan Fisher noted: "Every time Mrs. Jackson emerged from her car or was about to enter it, she looked up at the sun and threw it a kiss."

When the restraining order expired the following week, Marjorie telephoned Indiana National Bank and demanded $1,000,000. As arranged, she arrived in the parking garage behind the bank and went in and endorsed a check. Guards brought the money out in three bundles about three feet high and half as wide. With the cash in her trunk, Marjorie drove straight home.

The next morning, she showed up at Pfau's office.

"I knew God was on my side," she told the judge. Now, however, she feared the whole matter questioned her competence, and she worried something might leak into the newspapers. She wanted Pfau to write something attesting to her sanity and judgment. She had written herself a flowery statement, which she thrust in front of Pfau.

Sighing, he affixed his signature. "Now, will you do me a favor? Pick a doctor...."

"You're talking about a psychiatrist," Marjorie retorted, "and I'm not about to go to one. God is my physician, and that's all I need."

Six days later, she withdrew an additional $2,000,000.

This time someone followed her home, and Marjorie knew it. At high speed she went up Meridian Street, the main north-south thoroughfare, and crossed the yellow line to get around slower traffic. When she arrived at the gate on Spring Mill she jumped out to unlock it just as her pursuer pulled up with a screech of tires.

William Snyder, chief investigator for the prosecutor's office, flashed his credentials and handed her a piece of paper.

"Mrs. Jackson, this is personal service of a subpoena. You have to appear at the grand jury or be in violation of the law."

Marjorie looked exasperated. "Young man, why are you harassing me? I don't cause any trouble. Why do you keep bothering me?"

"We're just concerned about the money."

"That's none of your business." Marjorie blew a kiss to the sun.

Prosecutor James F. Kelley had been trying to think of any means to determine exactly what was going on. He had assigned investigators to watch her at the expense of their other duties. If there were fears Mrs. Jackson might be a victim of extortion, fraud or some con game, his people hadn't found a sliver of evidence. Still, Kelley and his advisers worried that so much cash would be a magnet for every crook, con man and slicker around.

When Marjorie showed up at the grand jury office two days later, Snyder greeted her and told her the prosecutor wanted to talk to her personally.

"Why do I have to see him?" Marjorie flared. "What are you people trying to do to me?"

"Once Mr. Kelley talks to you, that'll probably be the end of it," Snyder soothed.

On the elevator, Marjorie surprised Snyder by smiling.

"Hey," she said, "I gave you a pretty good chase, didn't I? Almost got away." Both of them laughed.

Her humor vanished the moment she entered Kelley's office.

"This is none of your goddamned business," Marjorie barked. Kelley and Snyder were surprised by her sudden vehemence and her language.

A handsome, dark-haired man in his second year as the county's chief criminal lawyer, Kelley steered her into a chair.

"Look, Mrs. Jackson, we're simply afraid someone is going to knock you over the head and take your money."

The officialdom of Marion County would do better to chase criminals than harass private citizens engaged in perfectly legitimate personal business, Marjorie insisted.

But, Kelley reasoned, if she had an accident while carrying a million dollars in cash and the trunk of her car popped open, money would blow around like invitations to every criminal in the state.

Marjorie sat up. "Do you know what a million dollars looks like?"

"I have no idea," Kelley conceded.

"It's about the size of a loaf of bread. I can put it in a bread wrapper. I can put two million dollars in two bread wrappers."

The meeting went on for a few more minutes. Kelley realized his hands were tied. They had no probable cause to do anything further. Marjorie left in triumph.

The next law enforcement officer Marjorie met wasn't local. Lee Mannen showed Marjorie his credentials as a special agent assigned to the Indianapolis office of the FBI. Marjorie seemed to like him immediately, partly because he was a mild, gray-grayed man close to her own age, partly because he was investigating Herb Biddle.

Mannen listened carefully as she told a story of plotting bankers and cheating lawyers. A shaky bridge of trust opened between them. Eventually, Mannen arranged a signal so Marjorie would know when he telephoned.

Mannen appeared to be surprised at what Biddle had done, perhaps because so many officers at Indiana National Bank truly were shocked. As the pieces of the puzzle fell into place, Mannen suspected he would have to arrest Biddle. Biddle had invested in bearer bonds issued by rural Indiana school corporations and designated the interest in his own name. It looked like Biddle had embezzled from other accounts as well.

On April 15, 1976, Biddle came to the FBI office and confessed. He had embezzled $625,000 worth of bonds from Marjorie's account, converted the interest coupons on other bonds, and destroyed some of the records.

Marjorie went back to the bank and closed her account, collecting nearly $3,000,000 in cash. In three months she had ferried a total of $7,880,671.74 in cash from downtown to her home.

She told agent Mannen the money was in a safe place.

ON a Sunday afternoon around one o'clock early that May, Marjorie returned home from shopping and suspected someone might be inside her house. She went to a black man for help.

Although Marjorie professed hatred for blacks, she made an exception for Jesse Lee Miller, who lived in the block of houses behind her property. A soft-spoken automotive worker, handy with tools, Miller occasionally did small chores for his neighbor. Marjorie apparently accepted him because he never complained about the condition of her yard.

Miller agreed to look around the house on condition that Marjorie allowed him to call the sheriff. Reluctantly, Marjorie consented. Miller thought the rear door had been forced open, but there was no one inside. With this news Marjorie decided she didn't want to summon the sheriff after all. "They have shamed God," she said, "and God will get even with them." Marjorie paid Miller twenty dollars for fixing the door and gave him a Persian rug as a gift.

A few days later, as she drove to the shopping center, Marjorie's 1955 Cadillac sputtered and stopped with a hiss of steam. A service station towed the car in, and the mechanic discovered a broken water hose. To his shock, Marjorie told him he could have the car.

The following day she arranged to inspect new cars at a Cadillac dealership. She selected two factory-fresh Sevilles, and paid cash. "I decided to get a brown one to drive in the winter and a white one for the summer," she told Jesse Miller.

On Sunday, May 16, Marjorie went shopping again. When she returned home just after six o'clock she found the rear door wide open. Her screams alerted neighbors, and two sheriff's cars arrived shortly. Reluctantly, Marjorie gave Deputy Mike Russo permission to enter the house.

A serious, dark-haired man, Russo had a fragile rapport with Mrs. Jackson. He knew the woman recently had taken large sums from her bank, but he understood she had deposited it in other banks.

Russo and a second deputy entered the garage. The floor looked like it had been scrubbed. Everything was in place except for a ladder. Russo climbed up. It looked like someone had used the ladder to reach the crawl space. He squeezed through a hole. His flashlight showed indentations in the insulation, as if someone had crawled along here.

Russo listened for a few moments. When he heard nothing he crawled over the beams until he found a hole someone had pounded through the ceiling. He stretched his head down to look around. Silence. He shifted and dropped through the hole.

Alice down the rabbit hole—into a congested, crazy place, rooms like part of a warehouse, or a museum. Russo glanced at the clutter, the impossible piles of bags and boxes, the stacks of food, the gleam of foil amid rich furnishings. There was so much clutter he couldn't tell if anything had been disturbed.

Russo checked all of the rooms. The intruders were gone.

"Oh, thank God," Marjorie said when Russo came outside. Now she wanted the deputies to leave, too. She didn't want to discuss any further investigation. She didn't want anyone inside again. She certainly would not cooperate with any detectives.

Marjorie offered the deputies money for their trouble. When they declined, she asked them to leave. "I'll be all right now," she insisted. "I'm just fine now."

When a detective telephoned the next day to follow up, she said she no longer cared about any loss, and hung up. The detective wrote in his report: "She was very belligerent and didn't want the police to come to her house. I am closing this case."

In fact, two young thieves had stolen more than $800,000 and some of Marjorie's jewelry.

4: BAD BOYS

IT was a burglary that begat a robbery that begat another robbery, a murder and an international manhunt. It was a caper executed by two amateurish high school dropouts who might have had to count on their fingers to spell caper. At times it resembled an outtake from *Dumb and Dumber*—or an episode of *Family Feud*. A sister betrayed her brother, a father betrayed his son, relatives schemed against relatives, friends plotted against friends.

And, by the end of this soap opera, just about everyone ended up dead broke and in court. Or dead.

The former divinity student

Jerry Allen Hornick, 26, was born in 1950 in Elkins, West Virginia, the fifth of eight children in a middle-class family. Five feet eleven and 185 pounds, he had brown eyes, brown hair and a beard. After high school he married and came to Indianapolis to study computer technology at ITT Technical Institute. He had one minor brush with the law, a charge of using a stolen credit card in 1970.

Hornick worked briefly as a computer programmer. With the encouragement of his sister and her husband, who were both ministers in Indianapolis, he went to Joplin, Missouri, to attend Ozark Bible College. He supported his family at the time by working as a service station attendant. He left the college when his wife became ill and they ran short of money. They had two children, a boy and girl. Jerry started drinking.

He got a job at a rental company and wondered how to get off the bad-luck merry-go-round of his life.

Later—much later—he would answer police questions.

Now, Jerry, this is in regards to the Marjorie Jackson residence burglary that happened on May 16, 1976. We want you to start from the start and tell us all about this burglary, who was connected with it and how the money was split and anything you might know about it.

Okay. Mrs. Jackson, I became aware of Mrs. Jackson's, say, irregularities through my brother that's worked at a flower shop. He was laughing about how she dressed, how she always on a Monday—excuse me, on a Tuesday or Wednesday—always purchased a dozen roses and paid with it with a $20 bill with a '32 year and...so, early in May I ventured up Spring Mill until I located her house, because there was only one on the whole lot that had the fence up over your head, plus the yard was just a mess. Uh, in the week before May 16, I come to Walter Bergin, Jr., in reference to a possible burglary at that home. I believe on a Thursday we parked the car down the street from it, walked down to her fence, jumped it, creeped up to the garage, looked in, there was two silver Cadillac Sevilles in there so we knew that was her residence.

We stayed in the yard approximately four to six hours waiting for her to leave. At that time we knew she went to church on Sunday, so later on, we decided that Sunday morning would be the time to do the burglary, because she would be out.

So we talked a little bit about it, what he was gonna do. My parting words to him, I said, "Well, if you get it done, drop by with some rent money." About five o'clock that afternoon Wally knocks on the door and, uh, motions me out to his car. Doug (Green) and him were in the car. He said, "We done it," and he told me the details about how they came through the garage up the attic, kicked the ceiling in and jumped through, and then he said that Doug was using one of her screwdrivers or a paring knife to pry open the doors and stuff and got a large case of diamonds and watches, and Wally in her bedroom found an attache case, opened it, and it had a large amount of money. At that time they told me they got around $80,000. They probably wasn't sure. He handed me two bundles of $100 bills. Each of them was $50 or $5,000. They were still wrapped in the bank wrapping. So the two bundles was $10,000.

Wally and Doug

Walter Berry Bergin, Jr., was a little guy, five feet five inches tall, 135 pounds, with blond hair, blue eyes, fair complexion, and an altar boy's smile. Born in 1956, he had a sister, Maywin, who was divorced and worked in a wig shop.

Wally's father, then in his early fifties, had spent two years at Purdue University studying metallurgy and was employed as a sheet metal worker for the Penn Central Railroad. Wally's mother had a beauty shop in their home to bring in extra money. Their residence was a pleasant brick and frame house, trimmed in black, in Heather Hills, a solidly middle-class neighborhood on the east side of Indianapolis.

Wally had had minor brushes with the law, usually with his childhood friend, Doug Green. He had dropped out of Warren Central High School. He got a job at a muffler shop, then at a tool rental company, where he met Jerry Hornick. Then he got a job as a warehouse stock boy.

Wally wanted money not just because he was stuck in a dead-end job. He wanted money to impress his ex-girlfriend, Judy. She had jilted him for a guy who claimed his dad was on the board of directors of Squibb Pharmaceuticals.

And when Jerry Hornick got a job at a Ford dealership and backed out of the Sunday burglary, Wally naturally thought of Doug Green.

At nineteen, Doug was strong and stubby at 5-8, 165 pounds, with an oval face, broad forehead, and shiny brown hair, parted near the middle and falling hippie-like down his neck. Thick and brown, his beard was lighter near the chin and along the moustache.

Born, like Wally, in 1956, he was the youngest of five children. His dad was a maintenance supervisor and his mother a bookkeeper. Like Wally, Doug had dropped out of Warren Central, lacking only five credits to graduate. He had had more than his share of scraps. In one fight he lost part of an ear. His criminal record included disorderly conduct and possession of PCP. He had been arrested once for burglary, but the charge was dismissed.

He had worked various jobs, including construction, before signing on as maintenance man at the Meadowbrook Apartments in 1973. His girlfriend, Donna Terry, just seventeen, lived with him. At the time, Doug claimed he didn't have enough money to marry her.

Sometimes, Doug and Wally talked about the future. What they wanted to do was to get a couple of fine-looking horses and ride them all the way to Canada. Later, he would have a story more fantastic than any adventure in Canada.

Doug Green's story

Then what happened?

Doug Green: Well, we tried several times to break in but it wouldn't break, and I told Wally that the house was break-in proof, that we ought to leave, and he said no, we got to get in there and get that money. I said how do you even know there's money in there? And he said because of Jerry Hornick. So back of the house was a round patio with glass slits in it, okay. I tried to jimmy those to get into the back porch, but there was no way I could do that.....so we decided to go into the garage. We tried the door and it was locked, and I stood back against the patio door and I took off running and I kicked the garage door and it slammed open. We went in the garage and there was a basement, so we went down there and there was no way into the house from there. And I said, "Hell, there ain't no way we can get in here." Wally looked up and seen a place to get into the attic, so he grabbed a stepladder and placed it underneath the hole. He climbed up and I went outside and hid behind a bush....Finally, he came out. He came out the back door through the sliding doors. So we walked into the house and the first room I walked in to was empty and I looked up and seen a hole through the ceiling where he had bashed and jumped down through.

Then what happened?

I said, "You jumped from there?" and he said yes, and we started, uh, went from that room into the kitchen. I was just amazed by all the groceries and

things that she had, you know, it was just, I couldn't
believe that one woman had all that. I said, "Hey,
man, what's going on?" So we looked around in
amazement mostly for about a half hour. We just
stood and stared, and we started going through things,
through rooms, and we spent about two hours just,
you know, looking at shit and picking up stuff. We
found a bakery in the back room. I mean, it was
actually a bakery, because she had all kinds of pastries
and fudge and stuff, so I started munching down on
pastries 'cause I was hungry, and we got out of that
room and I started walking into the front room, and it
was the first time I been in there, and I seen a piano
and the stuff she had in there, you know, and I stood
there and looked at that stuff for a long time.
Meantime, Wally was some place back by the bakery
going through stuff, and I walked from the living
room down the hallway, and as I was walking down
the hallway I seen a door in front of me and two on
each side, and I tried all the doors and they were
locked, so I went back into the kitchen to get a knife
so I could jimmy the door lock. I found a good knife,
you know. So I went back down to the doors and I
opened the door that we tried to break the window in
first to see what was in there, and I got the door open
and that room was completely empty. So I went to the
door directly across and I got that door open. I
opened the door and I just stood there and stared.
That's all I could do. I couldn't talk. I couldn't do
nothing except stand there and stare at that bed and
the tinfoil wraps on the side of the bed. It just totally

freaked me out, and I tried to call Wally's name but it was a kind of whisper, you know, and I tried to talk, and then finally, when I got my shit together, I said, "Wally, get back here, man, and look at this." So he came running down the hall and stood there at the doorway, and he said, "This is it." He had had a dream that night, this is what he told me, and I believe him, he said he had a dream that he had seen this bedroom with a double bed and a closet in the room, and he said he opened the closet, reached in and got out a briefcase, opened it up, and it was full of money. Well, I didn't believe him, okay? So I went over—he went in the room and stood there and looked at everything. I followed him in, went over to the dresser and started going through jewelry boxes and looking at the gifts, "To God From Marjorie." Man, there was a stack of them this high and they was full of diamond rings, watches, gold watches, all kinds of stuff, and I just couldn't figure nothing out. So I had a handful of watches and rings, diamond rings and stuff like that, and I put them in my pocket, and Wally got this briefcase out, set it on the floor, opened it up, and there was two burlap bags full of money.

Okay. Go on.

So we grabbed the sacks. We left the briefcase there and it was stupid. We should have took the briefcase, you know, any logical person would have took the briefcase. But we grabbed the sacks and took out the back door, and then I realized that we had touched a lot of things, you know, fingerprints. So we went back in the house and I rubbed the dresser off where I'd been, and the door knobs, and the knife that I used, I took it with me and I threw it in the back yard, uh, along with a lot of other shit. So I got back out in the back yard and Wally was kind of slouched down behind, beside this tree, and I grabbed the money sacks and took out towards the northwest corner of the yard. Okay, we had parked the car about a block away from the house....We hit the fence to leave. I had the heaviest money sack. Wally had the other one. He climbed the fence in a regular way. Well, I didn't hit the fence, and I rolled over taking the trees and stuff underneath me, you know, to keep my balance, 'cause I rolled over. I come out of the roll, I was over the fence and I had the money bag in my right hand. When I came down I popped my left ankle and it sprained it real bad and I couldn't walk....When I realized I couldn't walk or run, Wally was already halfway to the car by running, and I told him, I said, "Come on back here, I can't walk. Take this money bag."...We got to the car and we put the money in the trunk. We jumped in and went down Spring Mill Road. When we got to the creek I took the jewelry out of my pockets and I threw it in the creek.

How much jewelry did you throw in?

All I had.

How come you didn't keep it?

I didn't need it with all that money.

Now, the money, after you split it in your apartment, you thought you had about $400,000, right?

Well, it was a little over $400,000.

Well, how much did Wally have?
About the same amount I had.

After the Caper

Wally Bergin*:* Right after we did it we went straight over to Jerry's. Well, he knew we were going to do it because as we were driving over to Mrs. Jackson's place we saw him—he was driving down the road—and we met him and I told him that we were going to go ahead and do it, and he says okay but come by afterwards if you get lucky or whatever, so we came by and gave him $20,000.

Doug Green*:* We just handed him $20,000 and he was happy with it.

Wally*:* We went directly to Doug Green's apartment and then we split the money. We counted the money but we would not have an accurate figure on it, exactly how much we had. I mean, it was just split up. There was so much there we weren't really....

Doug*:* We went there and my girlfriend—she wasn't my wife at the time—had a girlfriend over and I made her leave, and brought the money in after she had left. Okay, Donna seen this money and she flipped out. She didn't want to have nothing to do with it. She stormed out the door and left me and Wally sitting with all this money. So once we had the money out of the sacks and on the floor, she came back in and I talked to her and convinced her to stay. She sat down on the couch and Wally and I stacked the money up next to each other....She sat there and watched us split it.

Donna Green: I think they got up to about $700,000 and quit, but I don't know. I can't remember....Wally got the big stack of hundreds and Doug got the small one, and they split the bills that were loose.

Doug: Then after Wally had left, I took my money and, well, I tried to count it as best I could, but I gave up 'cause I had never experienced that much money and I didn't know what I was doing. I just sat there and stared at it, wondering what the hell I was going to do. So I put it in a grocery sack and buried it. I kept a little stack of twenties at the apartment, about a thousand dollars. Well, I went to my cousin's farm and I dug a hole and I put it in there. When I got back to the apartment Donna was there and we just sat around and went and bought clothes, went out to a shopping center and bought clothes and stuff.

Donna: We went to Florida. We spent a lot of money in Florida. Daytona Beach, Holiday Inn and all that, and then he bought me a lot of maternity clothes and he bought himself quite a few clothes, and other than that I can't say there was much of a spending spree. I mean, yes, if we seen something we liked, we would, but we both held back quite a bit. I don't know why, but we did.

Doug: So time went on, about a month, and I went and dug up the money again. I got the money and I had it in the trunk of my sister's car. Judy Parrish. A red Capri. Well, it stayed in the trunk of that car. See, I didn't know what to do with it. Hell, I didn't know what to do with it, so I took it from that trunk and put it in the trunk of my Thunderbird, and it stayed there a couple of days. That was my car. It needed a transmission. So I took that money and bought a transmission for it. I paid him in $100 bills. I was working maintenance there at Meadowbrook at the time, and I went over to my sister's house, which she was living there, too—practically my whole family lived there—and when I walked through the door, she was sitting there crying. I asked her what was wrong, and she said her dude had left her to go to Australia with his first wife. I knew just the way to cheer her up. I went out in the car and got the money and come back in, and I said, "Look what I got." She goes, "What?" I said, "Just look in the bag." She goes, "What?" She bent over and looked in the bag and said, "Oh, my god, where did you get all this money?" And I told her. So I decided to keep it there.

Judy Parrish: He said, "Can I keep this here for a while?" He goes, "I think somebody's following me, and I want to know if I can keep this here." I think I just sat there, kind of in shock, and I said, "Where in hell did you get this money?" He said, "It doesn't matter where I got it." He goes, "It's cool." I said, "What do you mean it's cool? You're 'gonna get yourself put in jail." And he said, at that time he said it's not stolen. He said it's not stolen or it's stolen and it's taken care of, I don't remember which one he said, and then he said, "Well, can I leave it here?" And I said yes.

Doug: I decided to take it back and bury it again. So I went there one day and nobody was home so I let myself in with a pass key. I noticed that a good clump of the money was missing, but, hell, I didn't care, there was still more than I could ever do with, you know.

Judy: So in the meantime, Randy Parrish, my boyfriend, and I went back together, and Randy didn't know about the money at that time. It was hidden in my bedroom closet. At that time Randy and I was not married. We were planning on getting married and we wanted to buy a house, ourselves, so we talked to Doug. He says, "Well, with the money we could buy a house big enough for all of us." I know it was wrong, but I went along with it, and I said, "Well, if that's what, you know, if that's what you want to do, it's your money."

Doug: Not quite half was missing from my sister's closet, but it was quite a bit, you know. So I took the money out to Geist Reservoir and buried it. I know my way around out there because I used to hike there for the Boy Scouts. Well, I wasn't satisfied. I didn't want it there, so I went back and I dug it up. I was driving my sister's Capri at the time, 'cause I loved that little car with the four-speed, you know, and so I had the money in the trunk in a green paper bag. In the meantime, when the money was over at my sister's, she showed two girls the money. They were dykes, okay, and she used to go to school with them. So the next day, after I went back and got the money, well, it didn't stay buried but a day or two, the next thing I knew these two girls drove up in a brand-new red TR6 convertible, wanted me to buy it for them, and I said, "You've got to be kidding!" And she goes, "Well, you'll suffer the consequences if you don't buy it," and I said, "What do you mean?" And she goes, "You'll find out."

Doug and Donna Get Robbed

Donna: We had just come home from over at a friend's house and we walked into the apartment and just went to bed for the night. It was the day I found out I was pregnant. We went to bed and we heard a knock on the door. A guy had his finger over the peephole, and Doug thought it was my brother-in-law, so he let him in.

Doug: I just walked to the door and opened it up and these two goons were standing there. Next thing I know they were on top of me, and, uh, they wrestled me out into the middle of the front room. One of them was dirty as hell and I could smell his sweat and shit, you know, and the other guy was just as big and just as heavy, but he was cleaner.

Donna: I heard a bunch of racket, and then I seen them push him through the beads into the hallway and then punch him, and then he kept saying, "Where's the bedroom? Where's the bedroom?"

Doug: The commotion woke her up and she asked who it was. I said, "I don't know, I don't know." And they go, "Where's the money?" I said, "What money?" "You know what I'm talking about.

Where's the money?" I said, "I don't know what you're talking about." I tried to bullshit my way out of it.

Donna: They told us to lay down on the floor and we laid down on the floor. Then they let us sit up because my stomach was bothering me. They started questioning us. I finally told them the money was in the trunk of the car. One of them stayed in there and he had a little knife up to my neck, and the other had a gun and went out with Doug to the car.

Doug: The guy holding the gun said, "Okay, you've got five minutes to tell us where that goddamn money is or you're 'gonna die." I says, "Hey, look, man, I ain't got no money." I said, "Look, man, my girlfriend's pregnant." He said, "Good, she's the first one to go." So four and a half minutes went by and I'm still trying to bullshit my way out of it, and I said the money was in a safe deposit box in a bank. And he says, "All right, we'll wait here until tomorrow and then we'll go with you to the bank and get it." So that didn't work, so I said, "My sister's got it." "Okay, we'll go over there and get it." Son of a bitch was persistent. So Donna knew it was in the trunk and time was up. He brought back the lever, pointed it at Donna's stomach, and she goes, "It's in the trunk." He tells the other guy to stay with Donna in the bedroom and hold a knife on her, and he took me at gunpoint out to the car. I opened the trunk. He said he only wanted $50,000. I reached in to get $50,000 out, you know, and he grabbed the sack. At that time a policeman went round the corner and I looked around and I seen him, he was going real slow by us, you know. He says, "You make a move and I'll kill both of you." Boy, I wanted to flag that dude down. I didn't care, you know, about the money. So he went on by, and he grabbed a whole clump and went back inside, and as we walked through the door I could see the guy inside was standing to one side, and when he seen me walk in first he took out for Donna who was laying on the floor, you know, with this knife in his hand, and if that guy in back of me had of said it was okay, he would have stabbed her.

Donna: They tied us up with the sheets and Doug got untied and looked out the window and he seen the car drive away, and then he untied me and we went over to my sister-in-law's house, and he accused her because she had shown two dykes—I don't know their names—the money. We sit up there for a while and then nobody came home, so we went home. Then Judy confessed that she had taken some money from Doug.

Judy Parrish: In the meantime I have these two girlfriends. Well, one girlfriend, and her name is Linda (deleted). Linda lived in Kokomo. The other girl's name is Donna. Uh, okay, it was about twelve or twelve-thirty and Doug come pounding at our door, and he walks in and he says, "Somebody just held me up." He said, well, he didn't use those words but he said he'd been robbed. He thought that Linda did it because Linda was asking for some of the money. Linda had seen the money, from me, in the apartment. She had been my closest friend for a long time, I mean, we went through nursing school and everything together. She come over, and this was before Randy had moved back in, and I showed her the money, and she said the same thing, "Where in the hell did you get the money?" And I said Doug and a friend of his were supposedly got it, I don't know where it come from, all I know is that he said he got it. So, anyway, he come over and he'd been robbed and he said it was those two bitches....So I said, "Well, if you think it was them then we'll go down there." We drove to Kokomo and they weren't home, so we came back up and that's all I know about it.

A Report to the Police

On July 13, 1976, two women went to the Kokomo police to tell them about their friend Judy in Indianapolis, a twenty-four year old divorcee who worked as a $650-a-month bookkeeper at a finance company.

Two months earlier, they reported, Judy had shown them a grocery sack filled with money. Judy told them it contained $1,000,000. Judy's brother, Doug Green, had stolen the money from an old lady on the north side of Indianapolis who used to work for a bank and had embezzled the money. The other night two men with guns had stolen $150,000 from Doug and his girlfriend. Judy thought her friends were responsible and threatened to have them murdered.

The Kokomo detectives took careful notes. To verify some of this strange information, they arranged for Linda to call Doug's fiancee with a tape-recorder monitoring the conversation. They notified the Marion County Sheriff's Department, the Secret Service and the FBI.

The Secret Service had no evidence of any counterfeiting in Indianapolis, and embezzlement did not fall within its jurisdiction. Neither did the FBI have jurisdiction. The sheriff's department did, but everyone was busy with other cases.

The Kokomo reports were filed away.

The Farmhouse Feud

With the remaining money, Doug and his sister decided to buy a thirty-five acre farm in Jackson County south of Indianapolis. Here Doug and Donna and Judy and her then-boyfriend Randy Parrish all could live together, presumably happily ever after.

Parrish, a stocky former sailor who worked as a bill collector, was twenty-seven.

Randy Parrish: I don't know, you know, when I saw all the money it was bundles, you know, and, uh, I know Judy give him over half of it. I don't know how much was there because I didn't look at it. I just looked at it once, you know, and I said I don't want to see it again.

Doug: So, anyway, Judy told me that she had some money that she took out, you know, and I said, "Well, I knew that," but I didn't know how much and she wasn't going to tell me how much.

Donna: Judy was the one that had the money, and she would just give Doug so much at a time. I know that it was enough to buy a farm and, plus, I'd say about $50,000 more at least. She give him so much at a time, where we could live on, so, I mean, we were well off, I'm not 'gonna lie, you know, we didn't go hungry or didn't have, weren't able to do what we wanted to do.

Judy Parrish: In fact there was money in my apartment that he didn't take, because all of it wasn't stolen. The money was in the house and when he didn't have money he'd just tell me he wanted money. I wasn't really the keeper of the money. It was just there.

Randy Parrish: It was really before Doug told me that he had stolen the money. I said, well, I said Judy told me that she had some money. I said that I had some money, me and Judy had some money saved, $2,000. We was thinking about moving into a house, you know, buying a farm and moving out because it was a bad neighborhood and everything. They sat on the couch and he grinned, and he knew what was going on, and Donna knew. Then he said, "Well, I can put some money with it." I said, "Well, okay," and then it come to a total of $16,000. I said we can use our $2,000 and, you know, $13,000, and can buy a farm. I said, "You won't be able to get it in your name, because you're under-age." He was eighteen or nineteen; I was over twenty-one, and so was Judy.

Doug: It was in the newspaper. I picked it out and we all went down there, me and my sister and Randy and Donna. Donna didn't even go in. She sat in the car. It was late at night. The asking price was $45,000, I guess. Judy handled all of it...Donna and I, we were supposed to live in the house, but it didn't work out that way. We was actually kicked out of the house and down to the trailer, which was Randy's. Randy had the trailer moved to the farm so that he and Judy and the kids could live in the trailer, and Donna and I were going to stay in the house. Well, they accumulated so much shit that it wouldn't have fit in the trailer. The furniture, kitchen tables, you know, bedroom suites, all kinds of shit, and, well, Donna and I moved down to the trailer.

Donna: Judy bought too much to count. A six-room house full. I just know every time I would turn around there was a new camera, new piece of furniture, new this and new that....Judy is the type of person where she wants everything in her own hands. She wanted to rule the money and rule everybody's lives.

Judy: Well, we kept getting in arguments and everything over little stuff, you know. Two families can't live together, I guess. I don't know. Besides, Donna and I didn't get along. So, anyway, we kept arguing, so Doug was going to build a house on the farm, and we told him if that's what you want to do, it would probably be better that you did that.

Doug: See, I didn't have no cash at all. My sister had it. When I talked to the contractor and he, you know, laid the house out like I wanted it, he told me it would cost three grand to start it, to build the foundation and basement walls and stuff. While he was building the basement, uh, me and my sister got in a big argument. She was telling me that she didn't have any money. Well, I knew better. So, anyway, she finally told me that she had monies, but in that argument she took a .357 that wasn't loaded but she didn't know it wasn't loaded, and pointed at me and pulled the trigger a couple of times.

Judy: We finally got into the final argument. I mean I almost shot him 'cause I was so mad. I just could have killed him. It was always about the money every time we argued. I had had it. I just said, "That's it. I don't want the goddamned money, I don't want the farm, I don't want nothing. I just want to get the hell away from it." I said, "You're driving me up the wall," and I meant it.

Donna: They were arguing over money because we were worried we didn't have enough money to finish the house, and that's all we wanted was to finish the house and she wouldn't tell us how much money there was. She went to the gun cabinet and pulled the gun and pulled the trigger, but it wasn't loaded. So Doug gave her a gun, a shotgun, and she didn't fire it or anything, and they started throwing things around the house. Then she went to Indianapolis and got the money. It wasn't very much. It was just a little over $20,000. I think it was about $25,000, because we gave $20,000 to a friend of

Doug's who needed the money to keep his business going.

Randy: I just come home and Doug had been in the house and Judy and him were fighting and he had knocked everything off the kitchen table. And I said I'm leaving, and I left. I just left them down there and shit, and moved back up with my parents.

Doug: So after she did that I just wrecked the whole house. I have a violent temper and I just started breaking everything. But, you know, I didn't do too much damage. Just broke everything in the kitchen. So, Judy, she had taken $40,000 and given it to my brother, Danny. So she told Randy to tell me that the money was at Danny's, that I could pick it up there. I went up to Indianapolis and I got the money, and I went back down to the farm and I put the money in the trailer. I gave the contractor $10,000 cash. Okay, after that $10,000 ran out he needed some more. But one day I got a call from a friend; Kerry asked me if he could borrow $10,000 for his business, and I said yes, sure. I only had $20,000 left from the clump that my sister had given my brother. So I took the ten grand up there...I said when am I 'gonna get paid back, and he goes, "Well, within thirty days." Well, about a week passed and he wanted to borrow another ten grand. He said, "Don't worry about it, I'll give it back to you." So I counted it out and they didn't give me no receipt or nothing for it. He didn't pay me. That's why we had to borrow $20,000 against the farm, so I could pay the contractor. So I got the money to the contractor, and he just up and quit working on the house. He just never started work back on the house. All this time I'd been trying to get my money back from Kerry so I could pay the loan off, and there's been no hope. He just won't let up on it. He says he's behind in taxes and all this shit.

Randy: Winter was here, and that's when the arguments started, and Judy's brother Danny says, "I want you and Judy to come up to my apartment and we want to talk to you." I said all right. So we went up there. Doug and Donna was there and they wanted to know where the money was. Doug grabbed Judy around the neck and was choking her and stuff, and he wanted to know where the rest of his money was, and she said that she'd given him all the money, that was it, no more money, that was all of it. So Danny says, "Well, we don't believe you." I said, "I don't care if you believe me or not, there ain't no more money. That's it. We gave it all to you to give to Doug." So he said okay. He took Judy in the back room, Danny did, and talked to her, to see if she was telling the truth. Okay, she was telling the truth. So me and Doug and Danny went into the back room, and I told them, I said that was it, I was through with this whole thing, I said it's just driving me and her crazy. We were already married and I said it's just driving our marriage down the drain. So Doug says okay, we'll quit arguing and everything. So we moved back down there and it wasn't a week later that the house caught on fire.

Judy: I was in the bathtub and I heard a boom, like an explosion, and as far as I know it was an electric heater that had blown up. Everything was burned up. Everything.

Randy: So all we got was $40,000 insurance. We went down and paid off the mortgage loan, and we had about $10,000 left, and we, uh, went and bought furniture and moved into a place. I had the deed and everything, and I wanted to just give it to Doug and say, "Here, I'm through with it. It's yours." But he owed this contractor around $20,000. He didn't have no money and he expected us to give it to him. So I went down and got a loan and paid the contractor off. Doug would come around and he would want us to loan him money, and we didn't have any. He wanted to sell the place. I said all right, we'll sell it, pay off the loan down there. So when I started talking about it, he come over and said, uh, that the Mafia and all was after him....that they wanted the money and all of this stuff. I told him a thousand times to leave us alone about it, and he kept arguing more and more. So he got mad and he left. About two or three weeks later, he come rolling in there, said he didn't have a place to live, their baby was dirty, he didn't have a job, he didn't have nothing now, see, except his stereo system that he had, and his truck, and that's all he had. Judy told him, all right, you can live with us until you get a job and get some money and an apartment. Then she—his brothers and stuff, they acted like we were dirt, you know, that we spent all of Doug's money, when all the time Judy was giving him money, money, money. It didn't bother me because I'd just as soon get it out, and, you know, get it over with.

5: THE BODY SHOP

As the sticky web of stolen money entangled the Green family in greed, mistrust and violence, it slowly snarled the other young thief in a separate cocoon of avarice and betrayal. But the relative who took hold of Wally's bundles of cash wasn't a sister or brother; it was his father, Walter Bergin, Sr.

And two new players stepped eagerly onto the stage, Gary Perkins and Gary Walters.

The Two Garys

The son of a prosperous oilman, Gary Perkins was twenty-two and well-educated. He had taken classes at two small schools and earned a psychology degree at Kent State University. Although he had grown up in Ohio as the oldest child in a family of seven, he hadn't been able to settle on a direction in life, and had a minor brush with the law. He had just been arrested in Texas for possession of cocaine, and would get three years' probation as a youthful offender.

Wally Bergin didn't know this. The way Gary talked, Wally thought the man who had married his former girlfriend had the connections to launder his stolen money through Las Vegas.

Wally didn't particularly like Perkins, but he liked another Gary, Gary Walters. Gary Walters acted like he had his hand on the rump of destiny.

An acquaintance of Jerry Hornick's, Walters was twenty-four, short and glib, with brown hair cut over his ears and a moustache that made him look older. Pint-sized Gary had king-sized ideas. He planned to make millions of dollars by manufacturing a battery-powered car capable of traveling up to 240 miles without recharging.

In fact, Gary Walters had a title—president of Mechanics United Corp., a bona fide Indiana corporation, if largely on paper. The company had been formed to lure investors for the Car of the Future. To capture tomorrow's millions, some of today's thousands were needed. Wally liked Gary's ideas. Gary spent hours on the phone, supposedly lining up some Arab oil money or some connection to Arab money. Yet for the moment, promises and blueprints outweighed actual cash.

Gary Walters had an office in a small white house outside the Complete Body Shop, a new business in a barn-like building in a dreary industrial section on the south end of Indianapolis. While Gary worked the phones, Jerry Hornick worked in one of the four bays inside the yellow and cream rectangular building. He had invested in the business with $3,000 of the stolen money from Wally and Doug.

Different people came and went. Some of them eventually would hear wild stories that two kids had broken into a witch's home and stolen nearly a million dollars.

Father and Son

Wally Bergin: From Doug Green's house I went home. I left the money in my trunk. I did go to (my sister) Maywin's house that day. Now, I didn't tell her anything about the burglary. I just told her I had done something here. I gave her some money. I think it was $5,000. I went to bed. I woke up in the morning and told my parents that I was going to Florida, that I had a job lined up in Florida and I'd probably be gone for awhile. So that morning I went to Florida with the money. The whole thing. Probably $400,000. Maybe a little less, maybe a little more.

Did you go to Florida by yourself?

Wally: Yes. I stayed there maybe a month or three months, I'm really not sure about that. After I got back I stopped at home and checked in with my parents and sister, and told her that everything was fine, and the first thing I wanted to do was see my ex-girlfriend Judy. She had married Gary Perkins. I went to the Putt-Putt Center, where Gary and Judy Perkins were supposed to be, and we played Putt-Putt for awhile. We didn't talk about it then. We went to a restaurant and started talking about the deal. Gary told me that the money was not legal and that he could make it legal, through Las Vegas.

Did you tell him that you had burglarized Mrs. Jackson's home and that you had a large sum of money?

Wally: Yes, I did......so, anyway, he made a deal with me, that I was to give him $10,000 in advance for the paperwork, that he would go ahead and start the paperwork up through Vegas and get the money legalized. And, of course, I asked him what he would get out of this deal, and we really did not talk about it too much. He mentioned $30,000 or $40,000 that he would want. Well, the next day, I had given him $10,000, I went over to his place to show him the money. I showed him $200,000. From there we went to another restaurant and talked about it. He explained how he was going to make this money legal. Then I went home that night and I woke up, and, well, the money was missing out of the back trunk. So I went over to Gary Perkins' house and told him the deal was off because I did not have the money, which he was pretty sore about, and that my father—yes, my father—found the money in the back.

Your father is Walter Bergin, Sr.?

Wally: Yes.

Mr. Bergin: Well, Wally was carrying on about the money and stuff, and I still didn't have any idea that it was a burglary or anything. I just knew that he was having some kind of dealings, just the way he was talking about taking a trip and everything. I couldn't figure out just what it was, but I knew there was something bad going on, and if he was going to go some place to do something with any money, then I felt he was in danger. So, one morning—I get up early in the mornings—I'd say about three-thirty or so in the morning, I went out there and opened that trunk and felt around. Under that wheel there was a package, and I took it out. And that's what it was. All new bills. You could see they were marked in ten thousand packages. It looked like there was something like over \$200,000. The things that hold them together, I took those off and just threw them away. I didn't know what I was doing. I hid it in the garage, in one of those metal containers, one of those brown fire-proof boxes. I told my wife I burned the money. We had a barbeque pit out there, and I put newspapers on it. Of course Wally went out and checked it and he knew there wasn't any money burned in there. He said, "Well, you didn't burn any." I said, "Yes, I did, too." Of course I couldn't convince him. He figured that was just papers on there. Well, we went on with our plans. In the meantime, Wally was going back to work, for the body shop, but they had a big go-round over the contract. I thought, well, they're trying to help him out, see, so this is fine. I wouldn't say anything about the money. I just refused to admit there was anything, 'cause I didn't dare to. Whereas these boys were the other way. They just screamed their heads off about everything and it just scared me to death. 'Cause Gary Walters and Wally together, I'm telling you, they could make up more things than, I mean their imaginations were terrible.

Gary Perkins: Wally told us two different stories. One story was about an invention where he had made hundreds of thousands of dollars off of. Another story was that he talked to God a month or so ago and God instructed him to go over to a person's house to receive some money. Wally said God actually appeared in front of him and he talked to him. Wally said he went over to a person's house—he had to wear a special medallion to ward off evil spirits because she was a black witch and she would put a spell on him....Later on, Wally actually told us what basically happened, the truth about the burglary. He was going around telling us about the house, Marjorie Jackson's house, about her being a witch, and glass was bullet-proof, and only Doug and Wally knew how to get in, and he was telling us about the pianos in the house, the violin—it was a Stradivarius—and other miscellaneous things. Several months later, he said that they did burglarize the house several times after that. Uh, also he said he was working on his inventions with Gary Walters and Jerry Hornick, inventing batteries and battery-driven cars, all along showing that he did have money. He wanted us to come over just to show us how his apartment was furnished, new furniture and new stereo, and he said he paid straight cash. Later on, Wally then said he was going to enlist in the Navy, because he had been offered a position of making several million dollars from the Navy, and when he did get out he'd prove to us that he did make several million dollars.

Doug Green: Wally came over and told me that his dad had found the money and he was super upset, you know. I told him the news that I got ripped off. I told him that Judy had gotten some of it. So Judy gave me like $20,000. So Wally was out of money and him and Gary Walters was in on an electric deal—Gary Walters is a brain, I tell you, he is smart—so Wally needed some money, so I gave him like, shit, I think it was $10,000.

Mr. Bergin: I used some of the money for gas and a bit of running around and stuff like that. I didn't use much of it. I had no intentions of going with that money. Somehow I'd hang on to it some way, and I could take care of it later, you know. Now, to my boy, of course, he's going crazy with the money, so I have to say, "Okay, pad softly on these things," and go ahead and hang on to it the best I could. Go ahead and try to keep him out of trouble. And I kept him going. Put him in an inexpensive apartment.

Jerry Hornick: I had squandered all my money, this, there and drinking. Partying, really. I was down to about $4,700, and the last of May I invested $3,000 in the body shop, and it wasn't working out extremely well. First thing Wally said when he came back was that his dad burned the money, and I just couldn't hardly believe it. At that time he showed me about $7,000 under the bed. I told him about the body shop and he said he was going to have to invest in something. So he went out and looked at the body shop, and he was impressed with it, and he bought my interest out for $3,000. Mr. Bergin tried to get involved as far as helping and doing some of the paperwork and watching the paperwork like a hawk, making sure they was making money.

Mr. Bergin: They had written Wally up a contract on that body shop. They were going to make him a big shot or something. I stopped in there to look. It wasn't a big thing, but they had a nice business going. I talked to an attorney to get the contract straightened out, so I thought it would work out okay. Wally worked on that car and helped get that car going. Then they said, "Well, this car looks good and we ought to put it on the market, but we'll have to do some promotional work." So there's where I started coming in the picture. It was important to me because Wally was with it, and he had his interest in it, and I thought, well, since I'm starting my big enterprises up anyway, that would be a good phase to put in mine. It might cost a little money, but it would be worth it to get established in the procedures, and it was. I was hoping to get involved in promotional work on an engineering basis. I had an appliance repair course going, too. I had started it before I quit work at the railroad, and that was before any of this came up.

Jerry Hornick: I had got a job at a Ford dealership. Wally saw a car he liked and he took it out to let his dad drive it. They were both impressed. I believe it was a '72 T-Bird. We appraised his car, and it was about $4,000 difference. Mr. Bergin brought in $4,000 in $100 bills and the manager, he witnessed it being put in the safe. Mr. Bergin said not to let anybody else see it because we might get knocked on

the head. He didn't want anybody to know that he
had that much money.

Wally: Walters and I drove to Florida. We
stayed there awhile and then we flew back with our
car staying down there. It was a vacation and I had
heard that this electric car that we had, that Saudi
Arabia supposedly had found out about it and they
were worried about it. At the time I owned maybe
thirty percent, Dad owned maybe ten or twenty
percent, and Gary Walters or his mother owned the
rest. I had probably invested altogether probably
$6,000. We flew back, we talked about business, it was
nothing important, so then we flew back to Florida.
Then we drove to Mexico and stayed there a day or
two. Then we drove up to New York. We rented a
limousine one night. From there we went to either
Indianapolis or Maine, I'm not sure. We did go to
Maine. We stayed there a day and a half.

Gary Walters: We had a great time. He
showed me how to live. We went to Atlantic City,
went on the Boardwalk. It was kind of chilly, but the
beach was beautiful. We spent two days there. Wally
started to get depressed. I told him, "It's time to
move, man. You're getting a little bummed out." We
went to Manhattan. We rented a limousine. Gave the
chauffeur, right there on the spot, cash, about five or
six hundred dollars in $100 bills, and Dave
chauffeured us all around Manhattan, New York. We
smoked cigars and drank champagne. Dave said,
"Gentlemen, I'd like to take you some place very, very
nice, very sophisticated." We went to the World Trade

Center. It had crystal chandeliers and people who help you in the restrooms. We met two women and were riding around drinking champagne. We told them we were millionaires.

According to Walters, they went from Atlantic City to Boston, then Manhattan, then to Mexico via Texas. They partied whenever they could. Then they drove to Daytona Beach, Florida, where they continued partying. Their odyssey was interrupted when Mr. Bergin called and said Wally had to sign some documents. While they were in Indianapolis, Mr. Bergin told them Hornick and an associate planned to ask the Israeli government to invest $80 million in the electric car.

The two young men flew back to Daytona Beach. From there they drove back to Indianapolis, then to Bangor, Maine. On the return trip home, Wally told Gary about the break-in, and, Walters quoted Wally: "I trust you not just as a friend, but as a brother."

Connections to Murder

By the middle of the summer of 1976, at least ten people knew about the burglary—Doug and Donna Green; Doug's brother, Danny; their sister, Judy, and her boyfriend/husband, Randy Parrish; Jerry Hornick; Wally Bergin and his father; Gary Perkins, and Gary Walters.

The number undoubtedly was higher. Judy's two friends in Kokomo, for example, and the men who robbed Doug and Donna. Perhaps dozens of people heard the story. Certainly everyone who hung around the Complete Body Shop knew about how a witch lady who lived in a weird house on the north side had money lying around for the taking.

One afternoon, a new character showed up, a young man who had a gift for talking equal to Gary Walters'.

Ralph Wadsworth II drove up to the Complete Body Shop driving a red Triumph with a rod knocking. Hornick, who claimed he knew Wadsworth from his church-going days, introduced the newcomer around with some deference, for Wadsworth was executive secretary in the City of Indianapolis controller's office, although he was only twenty-five. College-educated and well-groomed, Wadsworth had been active in local Republican politics. He looked like a nice young man who would be comfortable leading a Junior Achievement meeting. In fact, he was anything but. Like a shark that never stops swimming, Wadsworth always had his eye out for anything to make money fast.

Wadsworth told Hornick he would be taking a part-time job at L. Strauss, a fashionable store in downtown Indianapolis, and the place had a safe containing maybe $50,000 or $60,000. Hornick laughed. He knew where there was a lot more.

Wadsworth listened in fascination. His old friend had fairy tales about kids stealing treasure from witches. Only this was no fairy tale. Hornick drew a map of the house on Spring Mill Road and explained how Green and Bergin had walked out of the place with a fortune. Who knew how much was left? Thousands? Millions?

Within a few evenings, Wadsworth and Hornick were driving to Spring Mill Road in the company of a body shop hanger-on named Dick, a wiry man who made Hornick nervous because Dick had a small-caliber pistol tucked in his pocket.

Under the cover of darkness, the men scaled the fence and approached the house. At the rear, Wadsworth cut the telephone lines. Then they saw cars in the garage and lights in the house, and retreated. Walking away, Hornick threw a rock through the garage window. It made him feel better.

By morning Wadsworth wanted to go back. Once again the three men approached the house. As they walked up to the yard, Marjorie Jackson suddenly appeared outside screaming, "Filthy animals! Filthy animals!" Once again, the men retreated.

These weren't the only attempted invasions. As events would prove, Wally returned to the house a second time, this time with Gary Walters.

The two young men continued their friendship, but the business relationship was crumbling. Increasingly, Mr. Bergin complained about his investment partners, the lack of progress, and the way Wally and Gary carried on when they went out to bars and nightclubs. Bergin told his wife the whole thing was more of a headache than he cared to cope with.

One afternoon, the former railroader noticed a car sitting in front of his house. After awhile he went outside and approached the driver's side. The stranger behind the wheel said he was waiting to see Bergin's daughter. He also wanted to see Wally. He said he was a private investigator trying to recover money from a burglary.

Bergin insisted he didn't know about any burglary, and asked the stranger to show some identification. The man started the engine. He told Bergin if he didn't come up with $100,000 he would be in a lot of trouble. Then he drove away.

A Man in a Bar

Then came a man named Willard. They called him Willie Joe, or Billy Joe.

Hornick: I met him at a bar, the Little Eagle Tavern. I was dating the bartender there, a waitress, and he was there with his wife. He come over to me and said, "Do you know any way to make some easy money? TV sets, just whatever you can get?" He told me he was an expert safe man. I took his phone number and told him I'd contact him later. I mentioned to Wadsworth that I knew a man that cracked safes, and he said Strauss had a safe that had fifty or sixty thousand dollars, so I set the meeting between Willard and Wadsworth, and told Willard to go to Strauss.

Wadsworth: This hillbilly guy came in. I just knew him as Willie Joe. He was dressed like a $2 pimp or something. He really looked raggy. He had this woman with him. We went across the street to this coffee shop and had a cup of coffee. We talked about this, that and the other, and I played little games with him.

Hornick: Later on that night, Willard and Wadsworth showed up and said they had went out and looked at the Jackson home and said it was a piece of cake. Wadsworth told me they picked the lock on the little gate and went in, looked all around the house, and that's what they were going to do. They was gonna go hit Mrs. Jackson again.

Wadsworth: There was snow on the ground and it was icy. We got into Willard's car and his wife or girlfriend drove. We talked about Mrs. Jackson as a witch who was into occultism or something, that she was capable of anything and might have a gun. Willard said, "I don't mind blowing the bitch away if she gives me any trouble."

Hornick: We had a hammer, a long pry-bar and a big screwdriver, and Willard said he was gonna pop up the garage door and go in that way. Wadsworth and him worked on the garage door. I stood in the bushes. They couldn't get the door up, and they made a lot of noise.

Wadsworth: Willard pried the garage door open about three inches. Hornick come up and said, "Come on, let's go. We're making a lot of noise." Willard wanted to keep on trying. He thought he was with a couple of amateurs.

Hornick: Then we left. He felt very flustered because of that, and he was still going to go in. Wadsworth discussed numerous other ways to get the job done. I believe it was a Saturday night in late December, we met at the body shop. Willard was quite drunk.

Wadsworth: Hornick and Willard had been drinking. Hornick accused me of setting them up with the prosecutor's office. Willard grabbed me around the throat and stuck a gun to my temple. He said, "You ever turn me in, you do anything to get me caught, I'll kill you."

Hornick: At that time he said for Wadsworth to meet him out at Wadsworth's apartments at one o'clock, I believe. We went out to the Jackson house. Luckily, someone had been there tramping around the trash. Of course, Willard knew then that something was wrong. He got quite upset with me because I let the kids—that's what he called them—get away with all the big money, and I blew that job.

Wadsworth: It was late at night, and Jerry was pretty drunk, and the guy scared me. He wanted to go back out there and look at it. I said okay, I'll meet you at the Waffle House on 86th street, and then I never showed up. I just went straight home and I locked all my doors and locked the sliding glass door that led on to the balcony, and I listened all night. I was afraid that guy was coming after me or something.

6: INVESTIGATION

ON a gray afternoon not long before Christmas 1976, Tommy Thompson answered the telephone.

As supervisor of Felony Screening for the Marion County prosecutor's office, Robert C. Thompson Jr.'s job was to establish in felony cases whether sufficient probable cause existed to issue warrants or otherwise proceed with prosecution. The job was one of the toughest in the office. An energetic fireplug of a man, his sandy hair usually awry like a schoolboy's, Thompson's voice fog-horned with authority. All too often he had to inform veteran police officers they did not have enough evidence to make a case, or tell angry citizens the law couldn't do anything to redress their grievances. It was heavy responsibility for a twenty-eight year old lawyer with two years of experience as a legal intern and a similar tenure as a deputy prosecutor.

Thompson liked his job. Most of the screwball complaints landed in Felony Screening, like the woman who described being paralyzed by fairy dust or the paranoid citizens who thought they were being followed by the FBI. Kooky complaints were not unusual.

"Well," the man on the phone began, "you're not going to believe this, but I'm a minister here in town, and I have a person that has come to me and told me he knows of a witch on the north side who can bury a dollar bill in the ground and dig it up a week later and it'd be a one-hundred dollar bill."

"Uh-huh," Thompson replied, suppressing his bemusement.

"Now, this person had planned with a couple of other guys to burglarize the witch's house, and backed out. But he got some money when the other guys did it—broke in and stole $800,000. What I want to know is, is there a possibility that if he comes forward he can get immunity?"

"I can't answer that now," Thompson told him. "Let me check with the prosecutor and I'll get back to you. You want to give me your name and number?"

The man identified himself and recited a telephone number. He was not, he added, a full-time minister.

Thompson decided a few telephone inquiries wouldn't hurt. Within a few hours he learned that the city police department, sheriff's department and state police had no reports of $800,000 burglaries. He decided to tell Prosecutor Jim Kelley anyway.

Kelley agreed the matter sounded interesting. He told his young deputy to pursue it further.

Thompson called the minister. The minister called back later to say the man would report to the prosecutor's office the next day. The following afternoon, Hornick walked in. "I'm here to talk about the burglary," he announced.

Thompson was surprised. Hornick certainly didn't look like the criminal type, the kind of informant he normally encountered. Hornick was close to his own age, well-dressed and groomed, with a beard and wire-rim glasses. He introduced a second man as Gary Walters.

"Would you be willing to give an oral statement?" Thompson asked.

"Yeah," Hornick sighed. "I just want to get this thing over with."

Inside a private room, Thompson started a tape recorder. Over the next half-hour Hornick related how Doug Green and Wally Bergin had broken into the home of Mrs. Jackson on Spring Mill Road last May and stole more than $800,000. He knew because he received some of the money, which he would be willing to attempt to repay. His friend Gary had gone on trips with Wally Bergin. Hornick talked only of the May burglary, omitting more recent events.

Walters came in next. His information did not seem as specific as Hornick's, but he had some tantalizing hearsay, including the story of how Wally Bergin's railroad-worker father had found Wally's share of the loot and burned some or all of it.

Thompson weighed the wild stories. If true, there was a crime and a fascinating case. Yet why were these young men volunteering information now, seven months later? Hornick claimed a guilty conscience motivated him. Walters said his friendship with Hornick brought him here. Still, Hornick had mentioned his investment in Walters's electric car project, and Walters acknowledged Wally Bergin and his dad also had invested. Did they want to squeeze the Bergins? Thompson wondered.

The young prosecutor sent the two men away with a recommendation to retain private attorneys. His next step was to track down a copy of the sheriff's report of the May 16 burglary. Attached to it was a supplemental report in which the detective quoted Mrs. Marjorie Jackson that nothing had been stolen. Thompson was puzzled. Maybe she didn't find out until later. If so, why didn't she notify the sheriff? It didn't make sense.

Gathering his information, Thompson scheduled a meeting with the prosecutor. Chief Investigator Bill Snyder sat in. As Thompson summarized the apparent facts, Snyder made the first connection between burglary victim Marjorie Jackson and the eccentric woman who had withdrawn millions from the bank in the winter and spring.

So, Prosecutor Kelley mused, Mrs. Jackson apparently did not put her millions in other banks.

Thompson listened with fascination as Kelley and Snyder recounted their frustrating meetings with the woman. But if Mrs. Jackson was kooky enough to disclaim knowledge of any theft, what then? You couldn't have a burglary without a victim. Kelley agreed, but instructed Thompson to keep working the matter. Maybe they would get lucky.

Thompson called the FBI. Agent Lee Mannen agreed an $800,000 theft was possible. He also agreed to telephone Mrs. Jackson using a special ringing code they had devised. For the first time, Thompson felt optimistic that a criminal case could be assembled.

Mannen called later. "Mrs. Jackson told me no money was taken. That anybody who said they did take money from her is a damned liar, and, since they didn't take anything, she's not going to prosecute."

Thompson took the information back to Kelley. "Let's continue the investigation," the prosecutor decided. "See what you can find out. Then we can show her the evidence. Maybe she'll change her mind."

They would have to proceed carefully. If the prosecutor's office filed charges against Green and Bergin and Mrs. Jackson failed to testify, every crook in town would pick her as a target. For now, they could notify the sheriff to keep a closer watch on the residence.

A few days later, as Thompson discussed the burglary with an assistant, another deputy prosecutor overheard him.

"Hey, I know about that," he said. "I got a report on this by a guy named Wadsworth."

LAWMEN tend to regard coincidence with a wary eye. Too often what looks to be coincidence is anything but, orbits of fact carefully shaped to look like they had no relationship. Yet Thompson was encouraged this time.

Wadsworth's name had surfaced a month and a half earlier during a fraud investigation unrelated to Marjorie Jackson. The police went to Wadsworth, who professed a sincere desire to cooperate. And why not? The young man was the executive secretary for the City Controller. And indeed he did cooperate, or apparently cooperated, giving a rambling fifty-seven page statement about people he knew, friends and acquaintances, all of whom, he insisted, were not close friends, close acquaintances. Good citizen Ralph Wadsworth II had wanted to help all he could, which proved to be not much. Yet as he departed, he threw in a bonus. Some kids had robbed an old woman named Jackson of a small fortune.

He wasn't very specific, and no one followed up. Now Thompson could.

The prosecutor arranged for Wadsworth to come in for a new interview. But after talking to Wadsworth, Thompson didn't know what to make of the man. Wadsworth was a strange bird, eager to be helpful, apparently sure of himself, yet somehow predatory in an oily way. My god, Thompson wondered, how did a man like this get such a sensitive position in the administration of Mayor Richard G. Lugar? He realized Wadsworth had a recent diploma from Indiana University, background as the enthusiastic chairman of the county's Young Republicans, and once had been co-chairman of the Mayor's Commission on Youth. But couldn't these people sense something shallow under the man's surface?

Yes, Wadsworth said, he'd heard about a robbery or burglary of an old lady. No, he had no first-hand information himself. Everything he knew he'd heard from Jerry Hornick.

Wadsworth promised to keep his eyes and ears open.

TOMMY Thompson felt grateful for the warmth of his office in the City-County Building. Outside, the first heavy storm of 1977 sent the mercury plunging to zero and below as a biting wind whipped the snow on the ground. It looked like an icebox winter, maybe the meanest in a long time.

Thompson answered the phone to hear Gary Walters talking with a note of urgency. Something was up. Mrs. Jackson might already be dead. There was a new man on the scene, Willard Something—they called him Billy Joe or Willy Joe. Walters had heard from Hornick what sounded like a specific threat. "They're going to go up there and rob her, and they don't care if they have to kill her."

Pulling out his file on the case, Thompson telephoned Marjorie Jackson's home. No answer. He called Lee Mannen at the FBI office and informed him of the new development. Mannen agreed to try to call the woman.

Mannen called back a few minutes later. Mrs. Jackson didn't answer her phone.

Thompson alerted the sheriff's department and called Aaron Haith. Haith was one of the investigators who had watched the Jackson residence the previous year. He had a gun and a car.

"We'd better get a woman, because she hates men," Haith suggested.

Thompson found a woman narcotics investigator who agreed to go along. The three of them drove north. The bitter January cold and a feeling of tension accompanied them. A sheriff's detective was bringing Gary Walters. Other units had been instructed to stake out the house. Thompson wondered if they would find Mrs. Jackson's body.

Haith parked behind a sheriff's car on 65th street. Footprints were visible in the snow near the northeast corner of the residence, on both sides of the fence. Several deputies, one carrying a shotgun, approached. The lock on the side gate had been broken. As they entered the property, Thompson joked nervously about his new life insurance policy.

The wind blew whirls of snow as they swung across the yard, making a wide arc to approach from the back. The glass-enclosed room next to the patio somehow looked eerie. Haith noticed pry marks on the garage door. They decided to swing around to the south side and try the front door.

Coming around the side, Haith heard someone yell, "Hey, it's a gun!"

A deputy cocked his shotgun as Haith dived behind a tree. Thompson couldn't see the deputies. He saw Haith running, and yelled, "What in hell are you doing, Aaron?"

"Can't you see she's got a gun?" Haith yelled back.

Thompson and the policewoman sprinted about ten feet to the shelter of a tree. Fully expecting shots to ring out, the young prosecutor felt his heart pounding. "And you would be talking about insurance," the woman whispered.

To Haith everyone seemed paralyzed for incalculable minutes. For the first time, Thompson heard Marjorie's voice in the crisp air:

"Get out of my yard!"

A door slammed, and someone said, "She's back in the house."

Thompson and the woman took the opportunity to run about fifty feet to the southeast corner of the yard and crouch behind a clump of trees. He could see a deputy near the south side of the house with little protection.

Suddenly, Marjorie's voice rang out. "I'm going to let my dog out! He'll get you off my property!"

"Don't worry," the nearest deputy said. "If that dog comes out I'll get him."

By now a deputy had circled back to the car for a bullhorn. "We're from the sheriff's department, Mrs. Jackson. We're not going to hurt you."

"Get off my property!" Marjorie yelled.

Thompson called out: "Have her call Lee Mannen at the FBI. He'll tell her it's okay."

After this Thompson decided he never had been colder in his life. Pain cramped his hands and legs. Next to him the woman shivered.

Finally Marjorie's voice rang out.

"All right, which of you is Mr. Thompson? I want to talk to you."

Shivering, Thompson fumbled for his wallet and got his badge in his right hand. "I'm Mr. Thompson," he yelled. "We're here to help you."

Approaching the front porch with his hands in the air, Thompson thought Aaron Haith was smiling as he passed him crouched in the snow. Thompson heard the click of a rifle or shotgun and wondered if he might get caught in a crossfire.

A tiny, silver-haired woman wearing only a flimsy housecoat, her hands jammed in the pockets, stared at him with a quizzical look.

"What are you doing here?" Marjorie demanded.

"Ma'am, we have a tip someone is going to rob your house. We called you on the phone and there was no answer. We thought you were dead."

"Then you come out here and invade my privacy. I'm perfectly all right."

Thompson shuffled his numb feet. Abruptly, the woman thanked him for their trouble and asked, "Where did you get this tip?"

"We have some people who came to our office. They think you have money in the house because of the burglary you had last spring."

"Well, they didn't get anything."

"We have someone who got some of the money and wants to pay it back."

Marjorie shook her head with disgust. "Whoever told you they took money out of my house is a damned liar. They didn't take anything."

"Would you prosecute if we can prove they did?"

"No, because they didn't take anything."

Suddenly, the woman mentioned her encounter with Prosecutor Jim Kelley, and complained about harassment.

"You know, you think I have a lot of money because of that Indiana National Bank. But there are other banks that take care of my money, and they don't have to be in Indiana."

By now the others had approached the front. Marjorie said the footprints in the snow came from trash collectors, and suddenly began ranting about Jews.

"Mrs. Jackson," Thompson interjected, "we have this information that some people are going to try to rob you. We'd like to give you police protection."

"Nobody is coming on my property. I don't need protection. If I have any problem I'll call the Meridian Hills marshal. I don't need protection. I don't want you here."

She offered Thompson one hundred dollars. He declined with the suggestion that they help her fix the fence gate. Marjorie brought a new lock and chain from the garage and watched, seemingly indifferent to the cold, as the deputies changed the lock.

"Well," Thompson said, "how are we going to know you're all right?"

The town marshal and Lee Mannen, Marjorie said.

Driving downtown, they laughed about the strange encounter. Thompson took off his shoes and held his feet under the heater. It felt heavenly.

Marjorie Jackson's gun, he remembered, was a cap pistol.

THE next day Mannen was not encouraging. Mrs. Jackson, he reported, remained adamant that nothing had been stolen.

While Thompson arranged for the sheriff to watch the residence, he felt mounting frustration. When he answered the telephone at home one night, he became even more puzzled. The caller identified himself as Gary Perkins and said he had married Wally Bergin's former girlfriend, and Wally had shown his wife money Wally stole in a burglary. Perkins seemed to be fishing for information. He didn't have any specific information himself, he claimed.

Thompson wondered. He had heard Perkins's name but knew little about him. He suggested Perkins could try to locate Bergin and persuade him to come downtown for an interview. Perkins said he would try.

Hanging up the phone, Thompson wondered exactly how many people knew about the May burglary. Wally Bergin and Doug Green, Jerry Hornick, Ralph Wadsworth, Bergin's father, Gary Walters, Perkins…Thompson suspected Perkins had heard about the investigation and wanted to find out why Hornick hadn't been arrested. Apparently he didn't know Kelley had signed a grant of immunity for Hornick on Jan. 6.

So far neither Bergin nor Green could be located. Wally supposedly had joined the Navy; Doug supposedly had a farm somewhere, no one knew exactly where. Even if they were located and brought in it was unlikely either would talk. And if they did, what then? Without Mrs. Jackson's cooperation the prosecutor's office had little chance of filing criminal charges that would stick.

The role of Walter Bergin, Sr., intrigued Thompson. If the older man indeed had some two or three hundred thousand dollars, as Hornick and Walters suggested, his financial records might yield telltale evidence. Bergin was a responsible citizen, with no criminal record. A grand jury breathing on his neck might compel him to talk.

Thompson arranged for a subpoena.

On Jan. 20, 1977, somber and nervous, Mr. Bergin, accompanied by an attorney, arrived at the grand jury office in the City-County Building. The lawyer waited outside as Thompson ushered Bergin into the grand jury room. It looked like a classroom, with a long table and a chalkboard bearing cryptic markings. The six grand jurors, all private citizens evincing varying degrees of interest, flanked the table.

Thompson read a waiver of rights. Bergin signed the paper, a gesture that he had nothing to hide. The preliminary questioning was routine. Thompson planned to work his way gradually to the question of the money. First he had to establish sources of income, a general financial picture.

Bergin appeared stonily determined. He said he had quit his railroad job and they were shutting down his wife's home beauty shop. He was uncertain what sort of income his son had; some money from working at the body shop, a little here and there. For himself he had invested in the electric car, but with money from his savings. The investment proved to be a continual headache. He estimated Wally had earned between $12,000 and $15,000 in the past few years, not counting money from the body shop and a job he had briefly in Florida.

Thompson said, "Now, are you familiar with the burglary at Mrs. Jackson's home?"

"I have been told about it."

"Who told you about it?"

"You did, on the phone."

"Did your son talk to you about it?"

"No."

Thompson pointed to a sign listing the penalty for perjury.

"Would you read that? Do you understand that?"

"Yes."

"Your son has never talked to you about this burglary?"

"No, he hasn't."

"You know nothing about the money that was taken in this burglary?"

"No."

Now Bergin remembered he had heard a second-hand story that some money, $200,000, had been stolen from an old woman, but he figured it was just one of the wild stories his son made up with his friends. "They go to the nightclubs and carry on all the time. That is the way I took it."

Thompson moved to another area, the report that a man came to Bergin's home demanding $100,000. Bergin conceded it had happened, although he said he couldn't remember details. He professed not to know why the stranger did such a thing.

"Did you ever talk to your son about this man coming to your house?"

"Yes, and his buddy, Gary, and they just said this is some goon or something. I said, well, I figured it was."

"When he said your son and daughter were involved in a burglary, did you question him about that?"

"I did tell them about that," Bergin explained mistily, "and they said there was nothing to it, nothing to it whatsoever. One of those people trying to make some problems, which, I believe, because these kids spouted off in those nightclubs constantly, and they were a threat."

It was a fairly good performance, a man willing to appear stupid or naïve, clearly lying yet giving just enough of an answer to avoid stepping into a trap.

Bergin's financial records weren't much help, showing neither significant income nor significant expenditures. Thompson told him he would be recalled later. But Thompson felt frustrated.

In fact nothing more could be done.

Thompson discussed all of the evidence with his Felony Screening colleagues and realized they had few options to offer Jim Kelley. Nothing in Bergin's records suggested that he had access to large sums. Mrs. Jackson insisted nothing had been stolen. The people who provided information were in the middle of a business dispute with Bergin. And, although Thompson believed a large sum had been stolen, they had yet to see a single dollar.

Hornick might testify, but he had none of the stolen money. Walters wouldn't be much better. Wadsworth had vague hearsay. At bottom no eyewitness could place young Bergin or Green at the scene of the crime.

Hell, no one could testify a crime actually occurred.

Thompson explained all of this to his boss. Going for outright burglary charges was out of the question. The only other possibility was conspiracy. Indiana law required a showing of an agreement between two or more persons and at least one demonstrable overt act. Hornick could not be considered a conspirator, because he had backed out. A conspiracy of theft might be possible but not much stronger.

If Green and Bergin were named in criminal warrants and the case failed due to the absence of Mrs. Jackson's testimony, nothing would be gained. No one could assert with certainty that money had been taken without her consent. And even if she did testify, any lawyer would easily make an issue of her sanity. If the case were lost she would be identified as a likely target for criminals throughout the state.

Kelley agreed. He told Thompson to keep the information on file in case something developed later. As he turned to other cases, Thompson had to shake his head at the irony.

Under the immunity agreement, Hornick had agreed to repay $10,000 to Marjorie Jackson, money she said wasn't hers.

7: THE WAITRESS

ROY Bettcher was a building contractor when he received his call from God. God told him to apply his talents to saving souls, and that's how Brother Roy became minister of missions for the Indianapolis district of the Church of the Nazarene.

During the Great Depression his assignment was to organize a church in every one of Indiana's ninety-two county seats, and in eight years he created twenty-five such temples. Then he became an evangelist and took to the road with a gospel singer.

Brother Roy preached the fire and brimstone theology of the Nazarenes. Among the instruments of sin were drinking, cosmetics, tight pants, fancy hairdos, moving pictures and cigarettes. Each day the Bettcher family—father, mother and five daughters—prayed for salvation. Where they lived, Mooresville, was a hamlet of a few thousand people fifteen miles southwest of Indianapolis past a series of eye-blink towns called Valley Mills and Tanglewood and Friendswood. On the occasions when Brother Roy took his family to the state capital, the highway seemed like a passageway to magic: faded farm buildings propped against the horizon, rickety farms with corn and soybean fields as far as the eye could see, and trains of the Pennsylvania Railroad racing along the side of Highway 67.

In the heart of the Depression, Brother Roy's oldest daughter, Marjorie, went to William Newby Elementary School. It was a big building on a bluff. Marjorie was an average student who went on to Mooresville High School. In her sophomore year she dropped out to get a job. She was fourteen when she went to work at Kelly's Drive-In in 1942. With her father gone much of the time, Marge—that's what everyone called her—experimented. She wore makeup, tried cigarettes, and dated boys. At Kelly's Drive-In she heard stories about love and sex which didn't seem to have as much to do with sin as they did with people just trying to make themselves happier.

Otherwise nothing much ever happened in Mooresville, which called itself the Home of the Indiana State Flag. The town was famous only for John Dillinger, who had lived on a farm outside of town, worked in the furniture factory, and played baseball at the county seat. Occasionally someone would stop at Kelly's for hamburgers and pie and ask where Dillinger used to live. These people thought Dillinger was like a modern Robin Hood or something, but Brother Roy knew better. Nothing but a no-good hoodlum, Brother Roy harrumphed.

Some day, Marge told her sisters, she would go to faraway places like New York and Los Angeles, maybe even as far as Europe. Yet each day passed with no more opportunity than the one before. She

was seventeen when she married Frank Spoon in
1945. When they divorced the next year, Marge
whispered to her sister Tina that Frank was like a sex
maniac.

Frank Knight, her second husband, was older
and more mature. Frank had the honor of marrying
the most popular waitress at Kelly's. They had three
children, but Marge refused to give up her job. She
dreamed about going back to high school and making
something out of her life. The marriage lasted twelve
years. They divorced once and remarried, and,
somehow, when a truck driver or salesman talked
about the world outside Mooresville, Marge didn't pay
as much attention as she used to.

In the late 1940s, Brother Roy, his wife and the
youngest children moved to Tennessee, where
Brother Roy became pastor of a church. From time to
time he would visit Indiana and talk about his ministry
and the tracts he wrote that attracted national
attention. He talked of Chattanooga and his married
daughters and his grandchildren.

He withheld comment when Marge and Frank
divorced the second time. Out of the marriage his
waitress-daughter had three daughters of her own.
Connie, the oldest, required psychiatric help. Donna,
the middle child, had a daughter who had been born
blind. At least Pam, the youngest, seemed normal.

Marge wondered about God and whether life
really was fair. How could it be fair when after all
these years she still worked at Kelly's, still waited on
customers and handled the cash register and smiled in

hopes the tips might be bigger. And she didn't have a high school diploma, one thing she wanted to get no matter how long it took.

These were some of the things on her mind when she married Robert Pollitt in 1970. Pollitt was a construction man, a gentle and good man. She was forty-two and getting married for the fourth time, with all of Mooresville left to conquer.

IT was a good marriage for the three years it lasted.

When throat cancer took Robert Pollitt, Marge reeled in grief. Taking stock, she realized she was a forty-five year old widow with three grown children, two failed marriages, and not much in the future. She had a nice white frame house on South Street with two wagon wheels by the sidewalk, Social Security benefits, a new trailer, and good health.

After the funeral, Marge went back to work at Mr. Kelly Poe's restaurant.

It was no longer just a popular drive-in at the south end of town. Kelly's had to change with the times, and the times brought McDonald's and Kentucky Fried Chicken and other fast-food places to Mooresville. Kelly's Restaurant had to compete with a growing number of rack-'em-and-sack-'em businesses along Indiana Street. Also Mooresville no longer could be called just a small town. By the early 1970s the population had nearly doubled, to 5,800.

It was like a little city hiding out in mostly rural Morgan County. In the big city they had busing of school kids and riots and traffic jams. Now many city folks moved to places like Mooresville. A lot of them were from Tennessee, Kentucky or North Carolina, many of them commuting to Indianapolis for factory jobs. They talked about the land and what was happening in the cities, and the Klan, and the black people who lived in the cities and wouldn't be real welcome in Mooresville. Just a few years ago, a black girl who came to nearby Martinsville to sell encyclopedias had been murdered, and no one had been arrested.

Working at Kelly's, Marge Pollitt considered ways to better her life. She wanted to get her high school diploma as much as ever. In her spare time she joined the VFW Auxiliary; Bob had served in World War II and was buried with veterans' honors. She sewed, crocheted rugs, and wondered how to improve her circumstances.

Over the months she wondered about getting a new man. Looking in the mirror, she considered herself attractive in a mature way, though given to a little weight now and wearing glasses as often as not. But she was lonely. She went out dancing and drinking more often, out to the bars.

Dancing one night to a favorite song in a friendly Mooresville bar, she saw a man sitting alone at a table. He appeared to be in his thirties, uncomfortable in a blue suit, not real tall but lithe and muscular, with wavy copper-colored hair, sideburns an inch above the neck, and his collar turned up like some country music star. He had a silk-thin moustache, blue eyes, and a suggestion of dimples. He looked like he didn't have a friend in the world.

"Well, smile," Marge teased. "It can't be all that bad."

He introduced himself as Howard Willard, and offered to buy her a drink.

Later, when she began calling him Billy Joe, after one of her favorite songs, she realized he really didn't have a friend in the world.

Quickly and completely, Marge fell in love with the man.

Nine years younger, he was not a large person, but muscular, coiled, and masculine. With his hairline receding, he had the front flipped over some, a cute waterfall, the sides slicked back shiny brown, the sideburns long and proud. The face tended towards thinness, the forehead high, the nose unremarkable, the eyes penetrating when they wanted to be. Handsome as a hillbilly prince, as some would say. Above his lip ran a thin moustache no more than a corn-silk shadow.

As much as Marge loved him, she hated the thing that made him weak, which was his drinking.

When Billy Joe was drinking there were times when they fought like wildcats. There were times when she went crying to Police Chief Kojak Martin. But as mad as she got, love always settled her down.

Divorced, an Indiana boy with country in his blood, Billy Joe told her about his boyhood, his family. His daddy had left home when he was five or six and his mother, Maggie Mae, remarried a factory worker to help raise the kids. Billy Joe's older brother and sister had married, hard workers with factory jobs, but he, Billy Joe, had trouble hanging on to a job because he had to drink to help wash away the pain and the headaches. As a boy he suffered rheumatic fever, and ever since he had a kind of nervous condition which, when it flared up, made his stomach crawl and his head throb.

The way Billy Joe told it, his troubles in the past really weren't his fault. As a boy he had had a few brushes with the law, and once the cops got your number they never let up. He had been in the state penal farm, even the state reformatory, for crimes he didn't commit. That's where he got his tattoos. On his upper right arm he had a star with his initials.

He moved into her house. South Street was in a quiet, tree-filled neighborhood three blocks from the center of town. Billy Joe got a job at a heating company in Indianapolis just before they were married in 1973. He always seemed to be there when she needed him, at first. When she went to the cemetery to visit Bob Pollitt's grave, he went with her and held her hand. When Brother Roy came up from Tennessee to visit, Billy Joe went to church with him. Billy Joe laughed when Marge sneaked out on the porch to have a cigarette; she didn't want her father to know she smoked.

The marriage didn't last six months.

As much as Marge loved the man, she had trouble coping with his darker side, with his drinking and his moods. The longer they were married the more he seemed to think he owned her. And they fought, screaming and yelling, until she ran out of the house and down to Chief of Police Kojak Martin.

Marge really didn't like Martin. She knew Kojak thought Billy Joe was nothing more than a common criminal. A peacock of a cop who went on TV because of the way he imitated actor Telly Savalas, his real name was Harold Martin. He had his head shaved, wore flashy suits and gold chains, puffed on dark-papered cigarettes, and showed people the letter he got from Telly Savalas which said how honored the actor felt to have the police chief of Mooresville, Indiana, borrow his TV name.

But she couldn't stay angry. Even though she divorced Billy Joe, she couldn't give him up. She drank a little more, went out drinking with him, and put up with his moods, hoping something, anything, would happen to change him. She prayed for a way to get him to stop drinking. Sober, he might get a good, steady job with better pay and not have to worry about money. He complained a lot about money.

It was crazy, Marge thought, that God made two people to live on such a roller coaster of joy and pain.

MARGE Pollitt's telephone call that March evening in 1976 didn't surprise Kojak Martin.

Over the past several years the chief had become accustomed to the domestic soap opera down on South Street. The complaints followed a kind of pattern: some godawful argument with her ex-husband, Marge heaving all of his clothes out on the porch, her sobbing lament that Howard Willard had smacked her or threatened to smack her, her promise to file charges, and, a day or two later, Marge's meek retreat, always claiming it was just a misunderstanding, they'd kissed and made up.

To Martin the whole thing was a circus. One time Marge actually had all the locks in the house changed, only to let Willard come back in a week or so later. How two people could live like that, well, the woman had to be dumb in love, that was for sure.

Kojak liked his job. His office reflected his own background and peculiar interests. Sixty-three and retired from the military police, he kept a photograph of Gen. Douglas MacArthur on the wall with the message DUTY HONOR COUNTRY. On his desk sat the framed photograph he had taken with Telly Savalas. Martin had even changed his middle name to Kojak. Although some people thought the chief looked more like Popeye than the TV actor, Martin enjoyed his small, local notoriety. He liked the town. Crime in Mooresville tended to be tidy and manageable. Criminals like Howard Russell Willard were the exception.

The funny thing was, Marge Pollitt refused to see Willard for what he was. To hear her talk, poor Howard was just an unlucky wayfarer who wouldn't hurt a field mouse. Kojak knew better. Willard's rap sheet showed the stripes of a career criminal: 1957, disorderly conduct, three months on the state prison farm, six months for burglary; 1958, a year for grand larceny; 1960, two months for filing a false crime report, then shipped to the state reformatory for parole violation; 1965, two to five years for second-degree burglary; 1968, two to five for safe burglary. Crime was in Willard's blood.

The chief was particularly intrigued by the 1968 arrest. Willard and a friend from Kentucky had been caught red-handed trying to bust into a safe at a Ford dealership over in the town of Plainfield. The Plainfield police had confiscated an impressive set of safe-cracking tools.

These records naturally made Willard a potential suspect whenever something happened around town. Just a low-life sneak thief with larceny in his genes, Kojak thought. There was no love lost between them, either. Rumor around town said Willard wanted to put out a contract to have Martin killed. What Marge saw in the man Kojak never would figure out. She just wasn't his kind, a widow lady well-liked in her circle, a fixture at Kelly's Restaurant. Kojak had met her father as well, a mighty fine gentleman.

On this Sunday night, Kojak climbed into his cruiser and drove the three blocks to Marge's house.

Greeting him at the front door, she showed signs of crying. She handed Martin a Regency scanner radio and told the chief she was pretty sure it was stolen. Kojak took the radio back to the police station and examined the serial number. It looked like it had been altered. Two days later, Marge summoned him again. This time she fetched an antique brass coal hopper from the kitchen cupboard. "I think it came from Kendrick," she said.

Howard Willard had been working as a maintenance man at Kendrick Memorial, the oldest hospital in town.

Within a few days Kojak verified both items had been stolen. With not a little satisfaction, he arranged for warrants charging Willard with receiving stolen property and removing serial numbers.

He could be forgiven a snicker of satisfaction at the opportunity to put Willard behind bars.

A radio and a coal hopper. Some big-time thief, that Howard.

SEVERAL months after his arrest, Billy Joe was picked up again, like a common drunk, for public intoxication. Then he got a job working in the refrigeration department at a medical center in Indianapolis. He was convicted of receiving stolen property and would have to go to prison for at least a year if his appeal didn't hold up.

Marge knew her father had been right about the evils of alcohol. Alcohol transformed people into monsters. Sober, Billy Joe could be kind, thoughtful, funny and loving. Drunk he turned moody, unpredictable, self-pitying and mean.

She was proud that he finally pulled himself back up, or seemed to.

He got a new job working maintenance at a country club in Indianapolis. He drank less, seemed to be in better spirits, and told her he loved her as no man had ever loved any woman before. He asked her to take him back, and she did. He was her man, always would be. Like an athlete coming out of a slump without being able to explain why, he took her dancing again, wrapped her in his warmth.

After thirty-four years, she quit her job at Kelly's. She went to Mooresville High School to take the GED test to qualify for a diploma. She talked with Billy Joe about getting a job as a keypunch operator, about going to business school, about changing her life around entirely. In October, they were married for the second time.

And then one night in December, everything changed again.

They went out drinking and dancing, and stopped at the Little Eagle Tavern on the west side of Indianapolis. Billy Joe fell into conversation with a stranger, a man named Jerry, Jerry Hornick.

Marge never expected to see the man again, but a few nights later Billy Joe told her to get dressed to go with him to Indianapolis to meet a fellow. When they arrived downtown, they went into L. Strauss Co. and Billy Joe met a man named Ralph Wadsworth. Then they went across the street to a cafeteria, and when Wadsworth came along she heard the two men talking about witches and a lot of money and a house anybody could get into.

Wadsworth agreed to show Billy Joe the house. As they followed Wadsworth's panel truck driving north, Marge told Billy Joe she didn't like the man. Billy Joe told her not to worry. All they were going to do was look at the place.

Fifteen minutes later, Wadsworth parked and climbed into Marge's Oldsmobile. Marge drove, following the young man's directions. Now Wadsworth talked about how two kids had robbed this witch as easy as taking money out of a church poor-box. They followed a winding road. Finally, Wadsworth pointed in the light of a street lamp as they passed a strange, eerie place set back from the street on a corner.

Wadsworth told Marge to drive around the block several times. Each time Billy Joe stared silently out the window. "Looks like a piece of cake to me," he said finally.

After that Billy Joe seemed transfixed, illuminated, caught up uncontrollably in the idea that something he had been waiting for all his life finally had arrived.

Marge sensed nothing could stop him. He was plunging into some kind of maelstrom, unable to stop himself, and as she reached out to grab him she might be pulled in herself.

Marge knew he really didn't believe this old woman was a witch. Yet she felt that deep inside him was an unspoken belief that there was something supernatural, or at least unnatural, about this woman, and, somehow, this was a sign in his favor. Besides, the knowledge that kids, mere kids, had robbed the old lady of a fortune made him shake his head in wonder, as if this were some kind of prelude, another sign of changing fortune for him.

Marge knew she shouldn't, couldn't go along. She couldn't stop herself. In the back of her mind a voice kept saying if she didn't go she wouldn't be there when he really needed her, indeed she might lose him forever if she wasn't there.

In late December she drove with him to a body shop on the south side of Indianapolis. Hornick and Wadsworth met the newcomers from Mooresville with a sense of anticipation. Everybody had been drinking. Sipping beer and whiskey, the three men discussed going to the witch's house. Marge smoked Pall Malls and bit her fingernails. Then she drove north with Billy Joe, following Wadsworth and Hornick. They rendezvoused outside an apartment complex, and Hornick and Wadsworth got into Marge's car. As instructed, she drove to the neighborhood and dropped the three men off in the dark. Billy Joe told her to drive around and pick them up thirty minutes later.

Marge turned one corner after another, watching the street signs with growing desperation. She was lost. Somehow, she eventually found the right street, and the three men scrambled out of a ditch. Billy Joe cursed the cold, their failure, and her tardiness. They had tried to pop open the garage door but it wouldn't open.

Marge felt like a fool. She couldn't live with the man and she couldn't live without him. Later, when Billy Joe began rambling again about the old lady and her money and the two punk kids who robbed her of a fortune, she refused to listen. The memory of the icy night in the car had to be blotted out until she felt certain it never happened.

She knew her love for the man welded them together so whatever happened to him would happen to her. She hoped the force of her own personality, her essential goodness, somehow could change him. But she had to fight his dark side, his obsession with the witch lady. Marge felt pity as well as fear, and when Billy Joe was fired from his country club job, for drunkenness, the emotions increased, for she knew he would have more time to drink and feel sorry for himself. In January 1977, she filed for divorce.

Still, she had to buoy him up, somehow. At the same time she had her own life to live. She got a job at the occupational development center in Plainfield. Her duties were varied, secretarial, helping in the kindergarten, assisting the nurse. As soon as she had enough money she planned to enroll in the business college whose advertisements she had clipped and saved. She had passed all four of the GED tests and officially was a graduate of Mooresville High School. Pretty good for a lady of forty-eight years.

Maybe her new job contributed to a change in Billy Joe. He started looking for work again and seemed to drink less. He began working around the house, fixing things that needed to be fixed, tinkering with hobbies in the basement.

As the weather turned, Marge wondered if the spring of 1977 offered the beginning of a new phase in their relationship.

IN April, when Eddie Stroud invited Marge and Billy Joe to help celebrate his forty-seventh birthday, Marge felt ready to party. She sensed a turning point, hoping Billy Joe could stay above his black moods and turn a new leaf in his life.

A friendly, robust black man, Eddie had worked in the cement business with Marge's late husband, Bob Pollitt. He knew how to have a good time, and he wanted to show the two white people some of the black hotspots in Indianapolis. Marge didn't care for the neighborhood at all, an inner-city street corner surrounded by haggard businesses, fading houses and storefront churches. The Shalimar Club itself wasn't much to look at either.

But the place throbbed with easy excitement. Soul music set a warm, foot-thumping tension around the tables and booths. The men wore immaculate, even outlandish suits with an abundance of chains, while the women, some wearing wigs, promenaded with sultry sensuality. Tipping his glass back and smoking, Billy Joe seemed to have a good time.

Everyone smiled when the slender black man glided over to their table, pointed a small camera, and flashed a toothy grin. "Hold it right there, folks," he said, and they posed as if having their pictures taken in an inner city bar was an everyday occurrence.

The young man sat down and melted into the conversation. He was chocolate-skinned, with thin hair and a moustache, probably in his twenties, and handsome in a tough way. His voice carried a sleepy cadence, throaty but smooth. Marge thought his name sounded Mexican or Spanish. Emanuel. Manuel. She never expected to see him again.

A few days later, Billy Joe called her at home and asked her to pick him up at the Shalimar Club. It took her quite awhile to find the place, and she was surprised to see Billy Joe standing outside with Manuel.

On the first Sunday in May, Billy Joe took Marge to River Downs race track in Cincinnati. Driving back into Indiana, he held the car well above the speed limit. "I had an appointment to meet Robinson at eight," he said, meaning Manuel Robinson. "I'm running late."

Such news did not please her. Billy Joe had told her Manuel had been in prison once. Still, Marge tried to be civil when they collected the black man at his mother's inner city apartment and drove to

Mooresville. Billy Joe and Manuel talked long into the night.

Marge went to bed. Monday morning she awoke and put on coffee. The sight of Manuel sleeping in her daughter's former bedroom startled her. A black man in Mooresville was looking for trouble. She woke up Billy Joe and told him to get rid of Manuel. Then she went to work.

Shortly after nine o'clock, Billy Joe telephoned her at the development center. She had to come home right away because of sickness in the family. He hung up without further explanation. Puzzled and worried, Marge made excuses.

When she pulled up outside the house on South Street, Billy Joe looked excited and asked her to come into the bedroom.

It seemed unreal. The money piled on the bed, crisp new bills in stack after stack, made her dizzy. Before she could say a word Billy Joe thrust several bundles into her hands and said it was $16,000.

Billy Joe grinned and told her he had inherited it. She could hardly hear what he said, his uncle in North Carolina who had been so sick lately—why would he expect her to believe this?

It had been a long time since she had seen her man so happy. In the instant of this realization was the knowledge of how much might be possible, coupled with the sudden fear that the police would pound on the door at any minute. When Billy Joe said he had $80,000, the numbers made her blink.

But she went along with him, yes she did.

They drove to Citizens Bank, right in the center
of town, and Billy Joe opened a checking account,
radiating a toothy smile as the teller made out the
papers. When the woman asked how much he wanted
to deposit, he tossed stacks of $20 bills on the
counter, a total of $12,000. A friend who owed him a
lot of money finally made good, he explained. "I
wanted to be paid in cash, and this is what he gave
me."

Next they drove to the savings and loan where
Marge had an account. She deposited $14,000. Billy
Joe opened his own account, putting in $3,000. Then
they went around the corner to Pat's Tavern. Over
drinks, Billy Joe talked about getting a new car. He
was tired of driving his beat-up eight-year-old station
wagon. He wanted a glistening new Lincoln, like big
shots had.

On the drive into Indianapolis he smacked his
lips at the wonder of the day.

"Me and Manuel hit it lucky," he said. "We
went to that witch's house. We just drove by, and the
witch was out in the back yard. She was talking to
someone. Hey, we just walked in and helped
ourselves."

They had $80,000 each, and the old lady
wouldn't even miss the money.

At Strickland Motors, Billy Joe picked out a
dove gray Mark V in the Cartier design series with a
price tag of $15,000. It had a moon roof, stereo tape
deck, power windows, cruise control, and a steering
wheel that tilted. He wrote a check for $12,000 and

paid the balance in cash. The salesman gave him $917 for his car.

By afternoon Billy Joe had decided Marge ought to have her own new car.

They drove back to Strickland and told salesman Dale Allison they wanted to order a Lincoln for her, and it had to have a moon roof. Billy Joe handed over $1,000 as a down payment. Allison wondered if there would be any difficulty arranging financing. "That's no problem," Billy Joe said. "I can get the money, everything I want."

THAT Monday afternoon, Manuel Robinson was looking for a new car as well.

At the Shalimar Club, the young man sipped a soft drink until a walnut-skinned man in his thirties approached. "I been looking for you," Robinson said. "I want to buy a car. Like to buy that Lincoln you had at your place."

John Williams had seen Robinson hanging around and knew Robinson had taken a liking to a Lincoln he had at his car wash. Still, he was surprised at Robinson's suggestion. No way Manuel could afford a Lincoln. Williams decided to chauffeur him to the Ford Motor Co. repossession lot ten minutes away. When they arrived, Manuel told him he wanted to buy a Lincoln or a Cougar, and price was no obstacle.

John Alton Williams was not a person to make
hasty decisions. Southern-born, the son of field hands,
he had hustled his way up the ladder. After living in
Chicago, where he clashed all too often with the law,
he married for the second time, a woman who wanted
to be a nurse and became a stabilizing influence in his
life. When they moved to Indianapolis, Williams
worked in construction and stayed out of trouble.
Then he got a job at a car dealership, earning upwards
of $300 a week, and bought a comfortable home in
the inner city. Eventually he opened his own business,
Johnny's Car Wash.

These things were not achieved without
blemishes. He had been arrested a few times for
drugs, once for possession of heroin, and for first-
degree murder. He claimed self-defense, the necessity
to send a shotgun blast in the direction of a man who
came at him outside the Shalimar Club. The trial
ended in a hung jury.

At the age of thirty-eight Williams considered
himself a success. He didn't know what to make of
Manuel Robinson. A lot of men from the
neighborhood had big talk and empty pockets. Still,
since he planned to drive out on the east side to pick
up a tire for his son's bicycle, he suggested Manuel go
along; they could visit a dealership on the way.

When they pulled into the Johnny Kool
Oldsmobile dealership, a yellow Pontiac Trans-Am
immediately attracted Manuel's eye. The salesman
wanted $7,200. Manuel peeled off five $20s as a down

payment. Looking at the thick wad of money, Williams decided he had misjudged the young man.

They drove back into the inner city and stopped at a dreary apartment building. Manuel went in and came out a few minutes later holding a paper sack containing three bundles of money. Back at the dealership, he handed Williams $7,100 for the balance on the Trans-Am. As a favor to Manuel, Williams had the car titled in his name.

It was a good deal. If anything happened to Manuel, the car would be his.

Manuel gave him a new $100 bill for his trouble.

TUESDAY morning, Marge telephoned work and said she wouldn't be in.

She and Billy Joe drove down to Pat's Tavern to relax and talk. Billy Joe had a mind to take a vacation, maybe go to Florida. They left Pat's and drove over to Billy Joe's ex-sister-in-law's house to show off his new car. Marge called Strickland Motors to cancel the order for her new car. When they drove to the dealership to have the turn signals on Billy Joe's new Lincoln fixed, she picked up the deposit.

The next day she slept late. It was a beautiful Wednesday, just starting to cloud over with signs of a front coming in. Billy Joe came into the bedroom wearing bib overalls, a checked shirt and a brown leather cowboy hat. He wanted to go to Pat's.

Reluctantly, Marge agreed. Her worst fear was that the money would lure him on the binge of all binges.

Just down Main Street from Mooresville's main intersection, Pat's specialized in neighborly company, good-humored kidding and regular doses of town gossip served up with beer or liquor. Virgil Huebner, the owner, was a bespectacled, middle-aged man with a pocked face and amiable demeanor. Howard Willard was one of his best customers.

Virgil was surprised when Howard came in with Marge Pollitt and asked, "Can I buy the house for an hour?" Virgil suggested a half an hour, and Howard handed him a $100 bill. He told Virgil he'd inherited a lot of money. Then he showed Virgil his new Lincoln.

While the bar owner was happy with their change in fortune, he kept an eye on the pair as they drank. But Marge was already trying to think of a way to lure Billy Joe out of there. Finally he agreed to take her home, and forked over $150 to cover the drinks, adding tips for Virgil and his bartender. He drove Marge home and disappeared in his new car.

That evening, Billy Joe drove his two-day old Mark V smack into the side of another car at an inner city intersection in Indianapolis.

No one was hurt. Billy Joe passed a sobriety test and hitched a ride to Strickland Motors to have the Mark towed in for repairs and pick up a rental car.

After dark he came home, looking sick and disgusted. He wanted Marge to go with him to look at the damaged car. Driving his rented gray Buick

Monarch up the state highway, Billy Joe stared moodily out the window. Before they left the dealership, he took some tools out of the trunk.

A slow, lazy rain began falling. Riding in silence, Marge could feel his mood darkening. Then she realized he had driven past the witch's house.

Billy Joe's voice had a hard edge. He wanted her to help him. He wanted to go in that house and get money. Marge was shaken. She couldn't, she told him in a meek voice.

He drove down a dark street which she recognized as the side street next to the witch's house. Billy Joe turned off the lights and told her to wait, then suggested she drive around the block. Then he vanished into the darkness.

Marge went around the block, returned to the side street, and parked. A few minutes later he came out of the dark and opened the door. "That crazy woman's got all the windows covered," he said. "I've got to find Manuel."

He drove straight to the Shalimar Club. Outside, he waved to a willowy young black woman and told Marge this was Velma, Manuel's girlfriend. Velma got in the car. As she slid into the rear seat, Billy Joe said, "Is that gun in your way?"

"No, I got plenty of room," Velma said.

Marge noticed the snout of the rifle sticking up from the seat. It was the Westernfield rifle her late husband owned. Billy Joe must have had the weapon in the trunk of the Lincoln.

He drove to an all-night chicken stand and got food for Marge. Velma said she thought Manuel was at the Zodiac Club, ten minutes or so from where they were.

Not many people were out past midnight, even in the inner city. The streets glistened with rain as Billy Joe followed Velma's directions. The Zodiac Club looked like a dive, but Billy Joe didn't hesitate, telling the women to wait in the car.

Marge felt funny sitting in the car at this time of night with a colored woman half her age. Cigarettes and small talk helped pass the time.

Twenty minutes later, Billy Joe emerged with Manuel in tow.

Slender and lithe, Manuel wore an immaculate yellow suit set off by a broad, sassy hat. When he took off the hat Marge saw he had shaved his head bald as a bowling ball. Now, in the dome light, she could see the cut scar on the right side of his face, the mole on his forehead. Diamond rings glistened on his fingers.

"You see what I got back there?" Billy Joe gestured over his shoulder at the rifle.

"Hey, where'd you get this, man?" Manuel said. "That's bad."

Driving through old, beat-up neighborhoods, Marge said as little as possible. Billy Joe broke the small talk.

"Man, I need some money," he told Manuel.

"Well," Manuel sniffed, "I don't know where we can get none this time of night."

"Man, we got something to do," Billy Joe said.

Marjorie Jackson Manuel Robinson

Marge Pollitt and Howard Russell Willard

Doug Green   Wally Bergin, Jr.

Jerry Hornick   Walter Bergin, Sr.

Gary Perkins   Judy Parrish

Randy Parrish   John Alton Williams

Robertina Harroll   Annie Young

Furniture outside front door after May 1977 fire

Prosecutor James F. Kelley watches Henry Gonzalez next to defendant Howard Russell Willard

8: MURDER & MONEY

JUST before dawn on May 7, 1977, the sky above Marjorie Jackson's home turned red and orange.

All along Spring Mill Road watchdogs and family pets began barking or howling. They were reacting to the approaching sirens of the Washington Township Fire Department and the brown and tan units of the sheriff's department.

When the first fire truck arrived the flames streamed twenty-five to thirty feet into the air from the house on the southwest corner of 65th street. Chains secured with padlocks stopped the firemen at the front gates. As they waited for bolt-cutters to arrive, Deputy Sheriff Charles R. Ellison looked at the burning house. He knew some of the stories about the eccentric woman who lived here. She hated people. She practiced forms of witchcraft. She had a fortune, yet scorned money with righteous wrath. And she was rumored to always carry a gun.

When the gates were opened firemen rushed up the weed-infested driveway. Flames crackled from the center of the ranch-style residence, shooting through the sloped gray-shingled roof. Three firemen pushed open the front door. While other firemen fanned through the burning home, Ellison circled to the rear. As neighbors gathered, staying back from the heat, he waved them away with his flashlight.

A glass-enclosed Florida room jutted out by the back door. The beam of the deputy's light revealed the door was ajar. Ellison noticed indentations on the casing. And some wires had been cut.

"Hey, I think Mrs. Jackson's inside!" a man cried out. A fireman's axe slashed through a side window. He could see the bed inside, unmade. Within a few minutes another fireman called out: "We've got a body in the kitchen."

Ellison went inside. Twenty-five feet or so from the heart of the fire, he stepped into the wedge-shaped kitchen cluttered with expensive appliances, overflowing with boxes and bags. The deputy gaped in surprise. Thousands of cookies and cakes were piled everywhere.

Flashlights illuminated the body. The woman lay on her right side, her silver hair matted, her face chiseled with an expression of perpetual surprise. Blood had streaked or dried on her skin, a frozen rivulet from her nose and mouth, a tiny pool beneath her. She wore a pale blue dressing gown over flower-pattern pajamas. Her right arm cushioned the body. The other arm, bearing a gold bracelet, rested near her face, as though catching a cough. No fire had touched her flesh or clothing.

The presence of death sobered the firemen as they did their work. They carried charred expensive tables and smoldering oriental rugs to the weeds outside. Other furnishings—gold and pink chairs, a baby grand piano, a Hammond organ, four TV sets, other things—were undamaged. Luckily the flames had concentrated in the main room, a kind of family room, where they had eaten through the floor, ceiling and roof. Yet smaller separate fires could be seen across the spongy blue carpet, suggesting arson.

The fire was subdued by daylight.

Within the smoking house something other than death imposed a creepy aura. The peculiar furnishings now created a palpable feeling of something unnatural, or unwholesome, or ritualistic. One by one, firemen and deputies followed each other's whispers to the dining room.

Here they saw a carved oak table arranged for a banquet suitable for royalty. Like a scene from some macabre movie, each setting had gold and silver china, Rogers silverware, ruby-glass goblets and candles whose smooth textures had been dimpled from the heat. Each setting had fruit, long ago rotted. Each setting had small, neat place cards. The cards lay next to foil packages containing rings, watches and precious jewels, including diamonds and sapphires.

All of the place cards had hand-written messages.

"To Jesus, from Marjorie."

"To God from Marjorie Jackson."

HAROLD Young rolled the stub of his Little Corona cigar on his teeth as he knelt next to the deputy coroner over the woman's body.

At fifty-one Young looked like a country sheriff. The Humpty Dumpty shape, the amply chinned face, the sensible spectacles, even the deliberate mouth encasing the stub of his cigar borrowed from or contributed to a hundred stereotypes of a country cop. The bulging coat, the polyester tie, the shiny black shoes were part of a dozen pieces of occupational insignia collected in several decades of police work. Young had been a detective sergeant for nine years, and by now murder had a smell as familiar as something overcooking in the oven.

At the moment the acrid smell of charred wood filled his nostrils. Young watched the practiced movements of the coroner's hands. The hole in the woman's abdomen looked like a gunshot, or the work of an ice pick, though they couldn't yet be certain. No exit wound could be found, anyway. Young felt some of the dried blood. The woman undoubtedly had been dead for several days, the coroner agreed. He moved the arms; the elbows were crooked, suggesting diminishing rigor mortis. The detective scratched notes in his notepad.

It was just after 8:30 on a Saturday morning. Neighbors had noticed flames around 6:30. Deputies had found evidence of forced entry. The victim, Marjorie V. Jackson, born Nov. 10, 1910, which made her sixty-six, displayed no signs of being touched by fire.

The prospect of a murder investigation stimulated Young's juices without particularly exciting him. Except in a crime of passion, when the wife or husband usually hands over the murder weapon, or a cheap punk murder, where a snitch usually is available, murder meant work. Long hours, phone calls not answered, tedious interrogations with a procession of liars protected by lawyers. Success might hinge not so much on whatever clues the house yielded as the ability of Young and his partner to parlay the best kind of currency a cop can get, information. Information from neighbors, friends, witnesses, informants.

And luck. Maybe they would need some luck on this one.

Young polished his tortoise-shell glasses and surveyed the surroundings. The first clues were in hand. Deputies found indications the chain had been snipped at a pathway gate on the north fence. A red and white can of brake fluid had been discovered in the dining room. Burglary and arson. Burglary, arson and murder. An eccentric woman living alone in a house almost designed to be burglarized. Yet there could be more. The place gave Young the creeps. The interior was like some strange museum in which who knows what dark theater had been enacted.

Obviously, much had happened in the master bedroom. Unmade bed, drawers thrown open, three chains dangling on the inside of the door. And the stuff thrown around the place—dozens of pairs of pajamas, so many shoes you couldn't count them, package upon package of pantyhose still in wrappers. Never in all of his years had Young been in such a bizarre place. Aluminum foil everywhere—on door handles, over railings, across windows, even the heat ducts. Young knew mentally deranged people sometimes used foil to repel alien rays.

It got stranger.

In the attached garage two of the bays were bricked up. Spotless new Cadillac Sevilles were parked in the other two. The ivory one had forty-four miles on the odometer, the brown one 2,610 miles. Shut off and apparently little used, another room contained dozens of bags of popcorn. The kitchen looked like a junkyard despite the Harvest Gold electric stove, two Sears microwave ovens, and other top-of-the-line appliances. The tile floor and counters were cluttered with cans and jars of peanut butter, honey, vegetables, hundreds of containers, enough coffee to supply a regiment. Plus dozens of loaves of bread, stacked like so many books waiting to be returned to their shelves. At least 2,000 cookies.

Still, the dining room topped them all. At the banquet table some of the fruit had been peeled, as if guests already had arrived. The packages of jewelry didn't make sense, either. And there weren't just watches and rings and bracelets. One package contained fifteen carefully folded Cannon washcloths.

Young heard another detective mutter something, and then exclaim in a rising voice: "Jesus, there's money lying all over the place."

Some of the sheriff's men had opened a ten-drawer vanity in a bathroom connecting the master bedroom to a smaller bedroom. Crisp new money filled each drawer.

Young opened the closet in the hallway between the bedrooms and kitchen. His shoe nudged a green thirty-two gallon plastic trash can. Leaning down, he lifted the lid.

"Holy shit," Young said.

The can was filled completely with money, thick bundles of money.

Other investigators swarmed in to look. Carefully, they transferred bundle after bundle onto a bed. Their nervous jokes faded away. They had barely made a dent in the bundles when they reached $600,000. There must be ten times that amount, millions, Young thought.

Someone found more money in the closet, five or six green toolboxes stuffed with cash.

The final tally would come later: $5,013,389.

Young wiped his brow. If millions of dollars had been left behind, what did the killer, or killers, steal? If Mrs. Jackson had been murdered several days ago, who started the fire during the night?

Young surveyed the bizarre surroundings. The house on Spring Mill Road surely had some strange tales to tell.

THE property was secured and the task of cataloguing evidence started. Photographs were taken and fingerprints collected, an inventory made, and the recovered mounds of cash, transferred to a grocery cart, put under the supervision of superior officers.

By mid-morning the body had been removed by ambulance, to be taken in for an autopsy. Samples of the carpet, rugs and furniture were carefully snipped for laboratory analysis. Looking for a murder weapon, the police scoured the home and grounds without success. All the neighbors were questioned; few could provide anything useful. One neighbor did observe that Mrs. Jackson's security lights were not on around 1:30 in the morning, but had made no inquiry. People tended to steer a wide path around the woman.

In the afternoon, an attorney showed up representing Mrs. Jackson's half-sister, Roberta, the widow of policeman Ray Koers. An estate had been set up on an emergency basis, authorizing the attorney to monitor the removal of any property. A rented truck was moved in to carry off valuables for storage. To the reporters and TV crews swarming outside the fence, fire officials estimated the damage at $100,000. Deputies had to direct traffic. Local radio stations were broadcasting news about the murder and some of the house's unusual contents—millions of dollars, plus other money. More than $30,000 stuffed in a chair, for instance, and forty-two $50 traveler's checks lying around.

Patiently, the rotund, bespectacled Young and his partner, Sgt. Harlan Rynard, marshaled their information. They had a lot of work to do. First on the agenda was Tommy Thompson. The young deputy prosecutor said he had urgent information.

Drinking coffee with Thompson in a nearby restaurant, Rynard made bird-track notes in his notebook. Rynard was younger than his partner, another veteran officer whose most prominent feature was his voice, a clear, booming baritone any radio announcer would envy. Like Young, Rynard expected a lengthy investigation.

Thompson's mind raced as he provided information. Mrs. Jackson's death had jolted him. Even more of a shock was the possibility that the teenage predators of a year ago might be involved.

Thompson listened as Young revealed how much money had been recovered. Mrs. Jackson had lied about what she did with the withdrawn millions. Thompson also wondered if enough had been done over the winter to break the old burglary case. Everything possible had been done, he thought; Marjorie might have signed her own death warrant by refusing to prosecute.

Now the young attorney recounted everything he knew about the year-old break-in: Hornick, the set-up man, Bergin and Green, the perpetrators, not to mention the perimeter presence of such characters as Wadsworth, Walters and Perkins. And there was

another name, Willard Something. They called him
Billy Joe or Willy Joe.

Young weighed the information. Maybe
someone had returned to the house for seconds. Now
they would start with Mr. Hornick.

No one answered the door at Hornick's
apartment. The detectives rattled the handle. When a
buzzing noise sounded they realized they'd set off
some kind of burglar alarm. Ironic, all right.

They decided to return later. The detectives
waited while Thompson called other prosecutors who
had talked with Gary Walters. But no one knew
whether Willard was a first name, surname or
nickname.

The three men returned to Hornick's
apartment. He was home now, and jittery after
hearing on the radio about the discovery of the body.
Young beheld a nervous, black-bearded man with
cold eyes. Hornick denied knowing anything about
the murder.

The detectives demanded an account of
Hornick's recent movements. Young had seen too
many Academy Award performances to believe
anyone the first time. Unlikely as it was that Hornick
had returned to the Jackson house after having
disclosed the first crime to the prosecutor's office, it
just might make good sense. Realizing the woman
never would prosecute, Hornick could have returned
for more easy plunder. The only flaw was that Mrs.
Jackson was dead. Hornick would know there was no
reason to kill her.

The former divinity student answered all of their questions. He insisted he hadn't seen Green, Bergin, Wadsworth or anyone else recently. Young began to think Hornick told the truth, maybe told the truth for the first time. Hornick's agreement to take a lie-detector test convinced his interrogators he probably had been out of the picture for months.

The detectives warned Hornick not to leave town. Next they drove to Gary Walters's house, arriving after dark. For a young man expecting to be a millionaire, Walters lived in modest circumstances, a quiet house owned by his mother in a suburban neighborhood. Another fast talker, Young observed, greeting Walters, who made a point of noting several times that he had warned Thompson months ago Mrs. Jackson was a target for murder.

Walters agreed to give a new statement on the old burglary, but claimed he could shed no light on anything recent. As far as he knew, Green lived on a farm somewhere south of the city, and Bergin had dropped out of sight amid talk about joining the Navy. The man named Willard might be anywhere.

Young shook his head as they left the house. He had seen Walters's type many times, a hustler with a high-speed mouth.

Not especially encouraged, the detectives drove downtown to the sheriff's office. Their desks in the squad room contained piles of messages. The autopsy showed Mrs. Jackson had died of a .22-caliber slug in the abdomen. The bullet penetrated the upper section of the abdomen, perforated part of the liver, duodenum and pancreas, and lodged in the back. Thus she had bled to death. The recovered slug would be relayed to the Indianapolis Police Department laboratory for testing. The pathologist had observed a small abrasion on the back of the woman's left elbow and a slight bruise on the left leg. As suspected, she had been dead perhaps forty-eight hours, which meant the murder occurred sometime Thursday night, May 5.

So the killer or killers visited the house at least twice, once for murder, again to set the fire to cover up the evidence. The arson people believed the brake fluid had been used as an accelerant in the foyer and near the dining area. But no particularly valuable fingerprints had been found.

The sheriff's department buzzed with news of what had been taken. Mrs. Jackson had withdrawn close to $8,000,000 from her bank, which suggested whoever killed her escaped with at least $3,000,000, maybe more. It was a big case, and the pressure to make arrests would start building up like a boiler.

The detectives grabbed a few hours of sleep and went back to work Sunday morning. Although they believed Green and Bergin had left town, they drove out to Heather Hills, only to find the Bergin family had moved, whereabouts unknown for the moment. At least they had a current address for Gary Perkins, an apartment complex on the north side.

Under questioning, Perkins was cagey and vague. Rich kid, twenty-four, good-looking, Young thought, and probably knew more than he was telling.

Misty about his own involvement in anything, Perkins said he didn't know what happened to Bergin but had heard he'd joined the Navy. He promised to call if he got a line on either Doug or Wally. Sure was a shock about the old woman. The headline of the morning's Indianapolis Star blared the news:

GROCERY HEIRESS FOUND SLAIN; BODY, $5 MILLION IN BURNED HOUSE

Young and Rynard returned to their office and began answering phone calls. The wire services had sent out a photograph showing a grocery cart filled with stacks of money, and reporters and TV stations from around the country wanted information. Other callers offered cranky notions and theories. Few of them had information to give.

Unless a break came fairly soon, unless someone made a mistake, Young figured there could be no end to the work in the days and weeks ahead.

ON the previous Thursday morning, Manuel Robinson showed up at Johnny Williams's car wash outside a weatherworn building off an inner-city intersection.

When Manuel told Williams he wanted to buy a new silver Lincoln Town Car, Williams wondered how the younger man could pay for it.

Manuel showed him. He went out to the yellow Trans Am and retrieved a suitcase filled with money.

"My ship came in," Manuel said. "Don't worry about it. Where I got it from they can't trace it or nothing."

The money came from an old widow's house where cans were stacked everywhere, he said.

He handed Williams $50,000 cash. "Go buy me a new car and keep the change."

Excitement and fear propelled Williams. He locked the car wash, drove directly home and called his lawyer. Then he drove downtown to the law office, taking three $100 bills and two or three $20s with him.

The lawyer examined the currency. It didn't appear to be counterfeit, and he knew of no major crimes in the city. Just taking money from someone else wouldn't necessarily constitute a crime, he concluded.

Williams drove to Crossroads Lincoln-Mercury on the south side of the city. Selecting a silver Continental out of stock, he put a $100 deposit in the salesman's hands while the car was prepared for the street. Williams drove home. When the salesman phoned later in the afternoon to announce that the car was ready, Williams had his wife drive him back to the south side. He forked over $12,104 in cash. The way he figured it, he was nearly $40,000 richer now than he had been in the morning.

When Manuel came to Williams's house to pick up the Continental, Williams learned he had done

even better. Manuel told him he could have the Trans
Am.

Saturday morning, Robinson returned to the
car wash. His new Continental had a scratch on the
fender and he was thinking about trading it in.

Williams invited Manuel to his home on
Sunday, Mother's Day, for dinner. On Monday
morning, Robinson returned again to the car wash,
saying he wanted to get a new Lincoln with a moon
window and sun roof.

Williams was more than happy to accompany
his new friend back to Crossroads Lincoln-Mercury.

In the showroom, Manuel saw a car he liked,
except it didn't have a tape deck, and he didn't feel
like waiting around for one to be installed. Williams
drove him to a second dealership, where the salesman
offered a new Mark V in exchange for Manuel's
scratched car plus $4,700. Manuel offered $4,000, but
the salesman wouldn't budge. Manuel told Williams
he wanted to go back to Crossroads.

The sales manager of Crossroads had spent
much of Sunday afternoon wondering if there could
be any connection between the murder of Marjorie
Jackson and the man who had paid for his new
Lincoln on Thursday with crisp new $100 bills. The
newspaper stories mentioned new money, new $100s,
plus the proposition that the woman had been killed
sometime Thursday.

On Monday morning, the manager telephoned
Duge Butler, the dealership's attorney. Within an
hour, Harold Young and Harlan Rynard arrived to

question employees. Only a few minutes after the detectives left, Williams and Robinson drove up.

The two men were oblivious to the tension around them. "We want a car with one of those cool moon roofs," Williams announced.

As the salesman tried to act as normal as possible, other employees alerted the sheriff's office. Robinson and Williams were shown various cars and told the kind of Mark V they wanted wasn't in stock. After forty-five minutes, they were ready to move on. By then five sheriff's units had them under surveillance.

The scratched Lincoln drove downtown, swung through an alley, and stopped in a no-parking zone within the shadow of the City-County Building. Through binoculars, detectives saw Robinson climb out and walk into a Mr. Dan's fast-food restaurant, where he bought a hot dog. Williams drove around the block twice and parked. Detectives recognized the man who came up to the car, a well-known criminal attorney named James Neel. Neel had an alarming question for his client. Was it possible any of Robinson's money came from the Jackson murder?

A few minutes later, Williams returned to Mr. Dan's, picked up Manuel, and headed north. About two miles north of downtown, the closest sheriff's unit pulled back, afraid he would be spotted. Moments later the radios started squawking; the Lincoln had disappeared.

Young and Rynard weren't worried. Crossroads Lincoln-Mercury had been able to identify the two men as John Alton Williams and Emanuel Lee Robinson. Already their criminal records were being pulled. The detectives also expected some of the money the men had spent could be traced. Only an hour earlier the FBI had received a Federal Reserve Bank list identifying the serial numbers of the millions Mrs. Jackson had withdrawn from the bank.

Sheriff's units staked out Williams's house and Robinson's apartment.

Unaware they were being followed, the two men had driven to a third dealership, looked at the stock, and selected two new Lincolns for a total price of $28,000. Williams peeled off three new $100 bills as down payment.

The manager wondered why anybody would want to trade in a new car with only 600 miles on the odometer. When he called Crossroads to ask about the other car, he was told his customers were wanted by the police. Nervously, the manager told the two men their purchases would have to be serviced, so they would have to come back later.

Williams and Robinson drove away. Both of them returned home.

Night fell. Sheriff's units were positioned at strategic locations in the streets and alleys around the Williams home. No one entered or left.

Finally, a dark Ford Galaxy pulled up. The horn honked twice. Williams walked out of the house and climbed into the passenger's side. A deputy with binoculars recognized the driver as Sgt. Harry Dunn, a detective with the Indianapolis Police Department.

Other units were radioed to move in closer. No one wanted a slip-up. Already Robinson had been spotted at his apartment, only to drive away with no one following because the stakeout team had been instructed not to leave. Luckily the scratched Lincoln had been spotted again outside the Shalimar Club.

About twenty-five minutes ticked away. Williams went back into the house and emerged wearing a hat and brown leather jacket. Dunn started the engine and drove west. One by one, sheriff's units fell in behind. Dunn turned south. The deputies figured he could be going downtown or to Robinson's place. Instructions crackled over the radio: stop the car.

Sirens whining, the sheriff's units swarmed around the Galaxy. Looking at armed deputies and detectives, Dunn identified himself, identified Williams as his nephew, and said he was taking Williams to police headquarters. Dunn watched as the detectives searched and handcuffed Williams.

YOUNG and Rynard were elated. The arrest broke the tension like an icicle snapping.

The news couldn't be better. Robinson was a convicted burglar on parole. Williams had a long criminal record. That the two would spend new $100 bills on flashy cars almost as if they wanted to attract attention seemed like a new record for stupidity.

The three interrogation rooms at the sheriff's office were grimy cell-like cubicles with fading green paint and one-way windows. Tables and chairs betraying the cigarette burns from thousands of hours of questioning were the only furnishings. Tommy Thompson joined Young and Rynard in one of the rooms.

The suspect hunched nervously over the table. To his interrogators he looked like a slick customer with his black moustache and goatee and darting eyes. Maybe he owned a car wash and had a wife and three kids, but he had a rap sheet showing arrests from heroin to murder.

Williams signed a waiver and promised to tell the truth. He answered the preliminary questions carefully. Yes, he knew Manuel Robinson, had been with him on Thursday, four days ago. He recounted buying Manuel a car and seeing a satchel full of money.

"What kind of bills were in it?" Rynard asked.

"Hundred dollar bills, $50 bills and $20 bills with bands around them. I did not see any markers on the bands. The bands did not look like they had no bank numbers or name or anything on them. They looked like brand new money, never been handled by anyone."

"So did you get any money from him?"

"He gave me approximately $20,000."

Rynard wondered what happened to the money.

"It went for a car, and he got the rest of it back. He got seven hundred from me today that was his money, and I have now, approximately, that I can give to you, three thousand."

Thompson said they would secure a search warrant for Williams's home.

"You don't need no warrant. Because I asked him from the beginning, I said, 'Boy, if you have done anything wrong, you know I'm in trouble now for something that some people's robbed me, and if you do anything wrong and involve me, I'm going to tell it.'"

Williams signed a consent form for his home to be searched, and wrote a note to his wife.

"Where is the money now, John?" Rynard asked.

"The money is there on the dresser in my bedroom, behind my baby son's picture. Man, it's brand new."

"Is there any more, John?"

"Hey, look. Number one, I'm going to be flat with you, man, because I don't go along with it. I don't go along with it, period. Not doing this, period."

Williams said Manuel had told him he and a white man obtained the money somewhere outside of Indianapolis. He recounted buying the Trans Am; Manuel had new $20s then, and later new $100s.

The detectives went over the car purchases again. Rynard asked how much the Continental cost.

"The car cost twelve thousand five hundred."

Then Williams should have $7,500, Rynard said.

"I don't have no $7,500 because I gave him eight or nine or maybe a thousand dollars back today. That is the truth."

"You have to tell the truth."

"I'm going to tell you the truth. I don't want no trouble."

While other detectives visited Williams's residence, Rynard and Young pressed the suspect for more than an hour. Yes, he had seen Robinson nearly every day. No, Manuel never mentioned Marjorie Jackson. Yes, Manuel gave him something other than money, some jewelry. It was hidden under the dog house in his backyard.

Finally, the search party returned and placed confiscated items on the table.

"Have you ever seen this before?" Rynard asked.

"Yes."

"What is it?"

"Hundred dollar bills. Came from Emanuel Robinson." A total of $2,000.

"Now, John, take a look at this and tell me what you have there."

"One rhinestone necklace."

"Is it jewelry?"

"Yes."

"Where did you get the jewelry?"

"Emanuel Robinson."

Outside the room, the sheriff and his aides consulted with Thompson. Sufficient probable cause now existed to arrest Robinson.

LEAVING the Shalimar Club in the spring darkness with a young, willowy woman as company, Manuel drove south in his new silver Lincoln. Seconds later, sheriff's cars swarmed around him.

The hairless ex-convict offered no resistance. Deputies found a pistol in the woman's purse. Her name was Annie Young.

At the sheriff's department, a detective popped into the interrogation room and announced, "We just got Robinson."

Young and Rynard were relieved. Now they could press Williams. Jim Neel, Williams's attorney, had called to say he had $1,000 cash Williams had given him. For all of his professions of wanting to cooperate, Williams claimed to know precious little about the source of the money.

A question asked a second time is a candidate for a new answer, and the detectives pounded their suspect with questions. Now Williams recalled Robinson told him he got the money "out of Indianapolis, in Marion or some town."

"In Marion County?" Rynard asked.

"In Marion County, those were the words he said. Marion County."

Williams claimed he'd told Manuel he couldn't afford any trouble because of his past troubles.

"Wait a minute," Rynard boomed in. "I want to know what he told you."

"He told me that he and a white fellow…now, I ain't ever seen him, ain't ever put my eyeballs on him or nothing…got this money. He said that there was some more there, so he must have gone back a second time."

Now Williams remembered Manuel telling him there was so much money he couldn't get it all.

"I'll tell you what he said because I want to help you all I can. I don't know nothing about it, and I can prove I don't know nothing about it. That's all I can do. I'll tell you because I want to help you."

"You're helping yourself," Rynard encouraged.

"I don't give a fuck one way or the other because I didn't do a goddamn thing one way or the other. If somebody give you some goddamn money, you going to take it."

At that he recalled another conversation. Manuel told him he got the cash from the house of an old lady around seventy. The woman never would report the theft, he quoted Robinson.

By now deputies were uncuffing Robinson in a room down the hall. His pockets yielded $2,202, including seven new $100 bills. He also handed over a diamond watch, silver necklace, and seven rings containing sixty-five diamonds. An eighth ring wouldn't come off his pinkie finger. Manuel seemed relaxed to the point of indifference. He insisted he had nothing to hide. Yes, he would be willing to sign a waiver and answer questions.

Segregated from her boyfriend, Annie Young, only twenty-two, was sullen and nervous. The pistol belonged to Manuel, she said, claiming she found it under his mattress. She wanted to help the police. She knew the location of a lot of money—in her apartment.

"How much money might be there?" a lieutenant asked.

"More than a million dollars, I think," she said.

She agreed to sign a waiver of consent to allow the apartment to be searched. Under the supervision of the sheriff, a search party was assembled.

Young and Rynard left the interrogation room and slipped into another one to question Williams's car-buying friend.

Robinson looked icy cool, a low-life who had been around the block more than once, the detectives thought. At twenty-nine he had been arrested a dozen times. Twice he had been convicted of burglary. Twice he had done hard time. His record showed he had been raised by his foster-grandmother in Mississippi, barely knew his father, and dropped out of high school. He was first arrested at age twelve, for petty larceny.

Sitting back from the table, Manuel answered questions.

Sure, he had a lot of money. A dude had given it to him, a white dude that he knew. The white man had dropped off the money for him to keep. The man's wife worked at a drugstore somewhere and found the money behind the place. Better than two million dollars.

No, he couldn't remember the white man's name.

Three miles away, a contingent of deputies approached Robinson's shabby inner-city apartment building. His mother, a thin, nervous woman, was surprised to see the police, perhaps not surprised Manuel had been arrested. She consented to a search.

The deputies fanned out through the uninviting, cheaply furnished rooms. A woman's diamond lay on the kitchen sink. A rifle sat in a closet. Beneath the bed in one of the two bedrooms was a brown suitcase. The top layer of $100 bills shielded a total of $652,000.

"Holy Jesus!" Manuel's mother shrieked. "How did all that money come into my house?"

After securing the apartment the squad moved down the street to the gray building where Annie Young lived. The manager unlocked her threadbare apartment. Again the deputies fanned out.

In the living room were new leather coats and other expensive apparel. Under a bed, a blue suitcase contained $645,079. A blue flight bag in one closet yielded $290,000. A total of $22,540 was stuffed in two drawers in a battered dresser.

The sheriff's men had confiscated more than $1,600,000 in less than an hour.

Downtown, Annie Young had added $560 from her purse. It was more than she collected each month in welfare checks. Young and Rynard questioned her. She said she had only known Manuel a few weeks. Until the previous Friday she'd spent little time with him. Then he came to her apartment.

"Was he by himself?"

"No."

"Who was with him?"

"A white male and a white female."

Annie said their names were Billy Joe and Marge, and she thought they lived in a city northeast of Indianapolis. Some time Friday night or Saturday morning, Billy Joe and Marge came to her apartment carrying suitcases and other things with money and jewelry.

"Do you have any idea how much money?"

"Over three million dollars."

"How did you obtain knowledge of the three million being in there?"

"Emanuel told me."

"Where did Emanuel tell you he got this money?"

"He said he stole it."

They went back to Robinson.

No, the suspect repeated, he couldn't remember the white dude's name.

"Hold it, Manuel," Rynard said. "All this stuff about the white guy, all this money, and you expect us to believe you don't even know his name?"

"He gave me his phone number. I got his phone number."

It was a Mooresville listing. Within half an hour the detectives knew it was registered to one Marjorie Pollitt, and her boyfriend and sometimes husband, Howard Russell Willard, was a known burglar.

Now Manuel had more to offer. He had been at this witch lady's house twice, once at night, once during daylight. Both times Willard had entered the house while he remained outside. Both occasions happened long before the woman was killed.

Rynard wanted to know if they had recovered all of the money stolen from Marjorie Jackson.

Robinson smiled. "I got a million stashed. If I go to the big house, I'll live better than you do on the street."

9: FUGITIVES

MURDER investigations, by and large, are tantalizing mysteries only in novels. In real life the average murder is no mystery at all. Most homicides focus on spouses, relatives, neighbors or drug connections, amateurs all and usually not very clever. Most of the time the killer ends up in jail through negligence, stupidity or bragging to the wrong person.

If the Jackson case hovered for fifty or so uncertain hours as a possible exception to the norm, the moment Young and Rynard were summoned back to Crossroads Lincoln-Mercury signaled the beginning of the end. Hour by hour, day by day, things fell into place. From that moment there could be no doubt someone would be convicted of something in connection with the murder. Exactly what happened, and who put the bullet in her, would be sorted out in due course, or so detectives believed.

Robinson was charged with first-degree murder, arson and burglary; Williams with being an accessory to murder, and Annie Young with possession of stolen money. Young became more cooperative. On the Thursday or Friday before the body was discovered, she said, Manuel had come to her apartment in the middle of the night with his white friends, Billy Joe and Marge. They were carrying boxes or suitcases which they opened up. The containers contained $3,000,000, and Billy Joe and Marge took half and left.

The next day, warrants were issued for Willard and Pollitt. Because of the probability that they had left the state, the FBI obtained warrants for unlawful flight to avoid prosecution.

To law enforcement, they were an unlikely pair of fugitives. Willard, thirty-eight, had been arrested twelve times since age twenty-two, twice served time for burglary, and had a star tattoo with his initials on his arm, acquired in prison. Marjorie Pollitt was something different. Nine years older, no criminal record, a divorcee and widow and mother and grandmother who'd worked for decades in the local restaurant, she didn't seem like the murdering kind. In interviews with detectives, her relatives admitted Marge would do anything for that no-account skunk of a boyfriend/husband.

When the sheriff's men obtained a warrant to search Pollitt's home, they found photographs of Pollitt and Willard together, pictures that soon would end up in newspapers around the country. With the front of his hair streaming over his forehead, sideburns plunging an inch below his earlobes, and a wispy moustache across his lip, Willard looked like a poor man's version of Elvis Presley.

Marge had the smile of a satisfied woman, with perhaps sadness in her eyes. Only her lacquered, ratted Petula Clark hair-do looked odd, like a helmet of hair. The house also yielded traceable remnants of burnt money wrappers, found in the fireplace. Local bank records told their story of the pair depositing large sums recently.

Interviews helped tie a ribbon around the potential prosecutions. A neighbor of Annie Young identified photographs of Willard and Pollitt as the people he observed early Thursday morning helping Robinson carry numerous items into Young's apartment. The FBI interviewed the car salesmen in detail. Marge's daughter, Connie, and her husband told the sheriff's men they had last seen Willard and Pollitt at about 10 o'clock at night on Saturday, the day the body was discovered. At the time, Willard was driving Marge's Oldsmobile with her Concord trailer hitched to the rear. They said they were going to Florida and would be back in two weeks. But, Connie said, her mother had whispered something to her. "She said that she would never see us again, probably."

From jail Johnny Williams continued to profess his desire to cooperate. During one interrogation, he told the officer that Manuel had money hidden on his person, in the jail itself.

Lt. Robert Kirkman ordered Robinson to come out of his cell and remove his clothing.

Robinson grinned. "I believe this is what you're looking for."

Reaching into his shorts, he pulled out a wad of money, then found more in his socks. Kirkman counted $4,200, all mint-new $50s and $100s.

"You're lucky I found out about it," he told Robinson. "There are guys in the cellblock who'll kill you for that."

"Yeah," Manuel said with a smile. "I'm sort of relieved."

Manuel's relief perhaps was not genuine. Four days later, he slipped three new $100 bills to a visiting girlfriend and asked her to buy money orders. Following a tip, the sheriff's men recovered the money hidden under a rug in her apartment. But no one ever would learn how Robinson managed to smuggle so much cash into his cell.

Under counseling of his lawyer, Williams agreed to tell all in exchange for a lesser charge of theft. He gave an extensive statement and led detectives to a branch bank where $40,000 was impounded from his safety deposit box. Williams also took a polygraph test. Although the examiner detected deception in answers to three questions, he concluded Williams told the truth when he said he wasn't a party to the murder, any burglary or any planning of the crime.

Williams met attorney Jim Neel in court, where his bond was lowered to $1,000.

"Are you sure $1,000 will insure his appearance in court?" the judge asked Neel.

"Your honor, my client would appear if you released him on his own recognizance."

"Yes, judge," Williams piped in, "I sure could use the hundred dollars."

The judge shook his head. "You've already used too many one hundred dollar bills, Mr. Williams."

NINE days after Marjorie Jackson's murder, Ralph Wadsworth II sat down in the interrogation room and watched Rynard start a tape recorder.

Understandably, Wadsworth was in a quandary.

The more he talked about Howard Willard, the more he might talk himself into a cell. On the other hand, he could hardly duck the police in a murder case, and he had to assume the sheriff's detectives didn't have the incomplete or misleading statements he'd made to Tommy Thompson.

Wadsworth had been released from his job with the City Controller's office and applied, unsuccessfully, for work as a civilian employee of the Indianapolis Police Department. Lately he had been working as a salesman. The front page stories bannering the Jackson murder had been a jolt. Hornick had warned him the police were looking for him. Now they wanted to know everything he knew about Willard, which didn't exactly put Wadsworth in a favorable light.

Wadsworth proceeded to weave a circuitous story of how he met Willard, a story in which Wadsworth seemed to be the hapless victim of plotting by others, as though he had innocently found himself in the wrong places with the wrong people. He described taking Willard to the Jackson house and returning a second time; he didn't mention other visits.

Young listened silently while Wadsworth rambled. To the detective, the young man projected something insincere and slimy. When the interview ended after less than twenty-five minutes, the officers said little.

Outside the room, Wadsworth agreed to take a lie-detector test. "If you lied or left anything out," Young told him, "you'd better think about it."

Wadsworth returned in the middle of the afternoon and wrote a statement by hand:

> The first time I was at the Jackson property was with Dick Schakel and Jerry Hornick. Schakel had a small caliber revolver. Upon leaving the property Jerry threw a rock through the front garage window, then we left. The next morning, Jerry, some kid and myself went back to the house. Mrs. Jackson saw us in the front yard and started calling us filthy animals, then we left. The third time was with Jerry and Willie Joe, as I have stated before.

So the web tightened. But where were Willard and Pollitt?

IF Mooresville Police Chief Kojak Martin was something of a colorful character emulating a TV cop, he was a mere peahen compared to the Marion County Sheriff, Donald Gilman.

"I might go down in history as a legend, the biggest high roller ever to be a respected cop," Diamond Don said. The sheriff did not mind the nickname; in fact he encouraged it. He wore gaudy diamonds and a vest embedded with diamonds. He drove big cars, flashed a wad of money, and in the vernacular of the day, he told it like it was.

He was as garrulous as he was vain. Stocky though balding, he was a high school dropout who had made millions running a chain of health spas and through gambling. He liked to talk about his trips to Las Vegas, how much money he made, and, with a shrug, how he had lost $30,000 one weekend.

As a businessman who contributed generously to the local Democrats, Gilman had been appointed to the sheriff's merit board. When Sheriff Larry Broderick, a friend, was killed in a traffic accident, the Democrats appointed Diamond Don to finish off the 21 months of his term.

Although his candor—some called it his big mouth—occasionally got him in trouble, Gilman sincerely wanted to do a good job. He sold his businesses and gave up, he said, his gambling pursuits. He wanted respectability, and he wanted to win the job on his merits in the next election.

On May 13, Diamond Don looked somber and authoritative as he called a press conference. Gilman knew the importance of the Jackson case. Reporters from as far away as Canada and England had besieged him for interviews. A Washington, D.C., television station had offered to fly his chief detective to the capital for an interview. At times the thing seemed like a circus. Diamond Don didn't mind the spotlight.

The sheriff read a statement for the cameras and tape recorders:

"This is an appeal to Howard Willard and Marjorie Pollitt to turn yourselves in to the nearest office of the FBI. This appeal is being made to you in the interest of your own personal safety and protection. Exaggerated stories and rumors that you have millions of dollars in your possession put your lives in great danger from unscrupulous persons.

"There is very little chance that you will escape apprehension, and there is a great chance that harm will come to you at the hands of people looking to gain whatever money you have in your possession. The serial numbers of all bills in this case are on file and can be easily traced. Again, Howard Willard and Marjorie Pollitt, for your own protection contact the nearest office of the FBI and surrender yourselves as soon as you can."

WHILE no one knew where the fugitives were, certain facts were being collected to establish their path of flight.

For example, not long after they left Indianapolis, Willard and Pollitt showed up in

Ringgold, Ga. Here Marge's sister Tina lived in a house made up of two back-to-back trailers.

Robertina Harroll was five years older than Marge, fifty-three, and not in good health. She had a nervous disorder for which she needed pills from the mental health clinic at Fort Oglethorpe. Married three times, once widowed and twice divorced, Tina had a daughter who lived on her own, a married son, and another boy, Timmy, only ten. She supported herself and the boy on her pay from a footwear company, where she operated a machine, plus Social Security and veterans' benefits.

At some point after the Indiana couple showed up, they left Ringgold, and Tina and Timmy went with them.

Not long after that, near Fort Smith, Ark., Marge and Tina entered a dealership and rented a twenty-six foot Winnebago. The dealer agreed to let them park their trailer on his lot while they were gone a couple of weeks.

Presently, the Winnebago arrived at the Safari Campgrounds, outside Phoenix, Ariz.

The place was a popular stop for trailers, motor homes and campers, and it had a swimming pool Timmy could use. Tina registered them, using the name Anderson, one of her ex-husband's names.

On May 17, in nearby Tempe, Marge's sister bought a motor home, paying $21,500 cash. The next day, driving the new motor home with her son by her side, Tina left the campgrounds, driving east.

That same day, in Indianapolis, Marion County Prosecutor Jim Kelley disclosed that a high-profile Miami attorney, Henry Gonzalez, had approached him in an attempt to negotiate the surrender of Willard and Pollitt. "I told him I don't negotiate with fugitives," Kelley said.

On May 19, a man and woman drove into Bill Moore Motor Homes in Tempe, the same place where Marge's sister had been a few days before. The couple selected a thirty-three foot Fore Travel motor home, specifying that it had to have a double bed in back, a TV set, and a small table between the front seats. The man filled out the papers, using the name Robert Rollitt, Jr.

With a purchase price of $35,515, salesman Bob Humburg was pleased. How did they intend to pay?

"Cash," the man said.

"You mean cash money? Greenbacks?"

Yes, the man said.

Humburg told them he'd have the unit ready within a few hours. At seven o'clock that evening the couple returned, and the man counted out the thousands in $100 bills.

Something wasn't right, Humburg decided. Humburg excused himself and went to talk to the manager. Then he told the mechanic to disable the unit so it wouldn't start, and returned to the showroom. The unit wouldn't be ready until morning, he announced. The dealership would be happy to pay for an overnight motel room for Mr. and Mrs. Rollitt. The man said they'd be back in the morning.

Tempe police were notified. A detective came over to interview Humburg. He brought along a photograph of Marge Pollitt. Yes, Humburg said, she appeared to be the same woman.

The morning of May 20 arrived cloudless and blue. At the Safari Campgrounds, an FBI agent was interviewing the manager when a man walked up to use the public telephone. He wore a light gray shirt, gray slacks and Western-style hat.

As he dialed a number, the agent tapped him on the shoulder and flashed credentials.

"FBI. We're working on a fugitive case, looking for Howard Russell Willard. Can I see some identification?"

The man opened his wallet. "Am I under arrest?"

"We're looking for Howard Russell Willard." Another FBI agent approached. More were moving in the background.

"Well, I'm not Willard, so this doesn't concern me."

"How old are you?"

"Forty-seven." Willard couldn't remember the date of birth on Bob Pollitt's altered driver's license.

The agent asked him to roll up his sleeve. As he did so, the agent pushed it higher. The star tattoo and initials were like a brand.

"Are you Willard?"

"No."

The agents escorted him to an FBI car. Everything could be settled if he would come to the FBI office for fingerprinting. Willard asked if he could get a cold beer. He saw more FBI cars pulling up.

They spread-eagled and frisked him before snapping handcuffs on his wrists and shoving him into the back seat.

"Where's Marjorie Pollitt?"

The suspect sighed. "Marjorie is in the Winnebago and Robertina is on her way home."

"You mean on her way to Georgia?"

"I said she is on her way home."

"Are you Willard?"

He didn't answer. Then he asked if he could get Marge, because she was alone in the motor home and armed with a gas gun. The agents refused.

About a dozen agents and officers surrounded the Winnebago. Someone knocked on the door.

"FBI! Come out with your hands up!"

Peeking through the window, the former Mooresville waitress felt sick to her stomach and slumped to the floor. Then a voice which sounded like it was on the radio announced that Howard Willard was in custody.

She opened the door and walked outside.

A search of the motor home and rented car turned up $170,745 cash, various other kinds of evidence—and a shovel.

Four days later, Robertina was arrested at a trailer park near Atlanta. A total of $142,000 cash was found in her mobile home and $4,604 in her purse.

Painted in yellow and institutional gray, the county jail was depressing.

The days dragged by under a dark cloud from which Marge Pollitt could not escape, a dull malaise engulfing her. To fill the time as much as anything, she prayed a lot, prayed on her hands and knees as she did when she was a little girl under the exhortations of her father. She came to believe that God listened to her, that God made the warts disappear from her hands. When she didn't pray or sleep she wrote letters, to her sisters, to her parents, to Billy Joe's relatives. Writing helped her to forget how much she stood to lose. Her home, her trailer, her freedom, her man, everything. Ahead lay prison, a kind of death for no matter how long she lived.

"I'm worried about Billy Joe," she wrote to his sister. "I know in my heart your brother didn't do all of those things their accusing him of. The time I've lived with him I feel that I know him better than anyone else. He couldn't and wouldn't be mean or harm a dumb animal, let alone a human being. Don't ever believe that he killed that woman. You and I know he wouldn't. He evidently met up with the wrong person this time. My sister and I have suffered a lot from this ordeal. But we neither one believe Billy Joe is guilty."

Marge had been secluded in a rural jail away from Indianapolis. The few other prisoners weren't much to talk to, common criminals or hard-luck cases with stories of ill fortune. Her own story carried a certain fascination, how a simple small-town waitress got swept up in a million-dollar murder scandal.

Since her arrest everything had happened quickly: the Arizona jail, the appearance before a federal magistrate, the plane ride home in handcuffs, going to federal court with reporters staring curiously and the magistrates and judges looking aloof and distant. She found out the motor home dealer had called the police. Poor Tina had been arrested as well. What would happen to Tina? To Timmy? A federal grand jury had indicted Marge and Billy Joe for interstate transportation of stolen money, and Tina stood accused of abetting them. When the judge raised their bond to $5,000,000 each, the number seemed beyond comprehension, though she had seen almost as much in the past weeks.

One surprise, that the famous lawyer F. Lee Bailey wouldn't be their attorney. When Henry Gonzalez came to visit her in jail, he had another lawyer with him, Jim Voyles, from Indianapolis. Voyles was a black-haired, soft-spoken man in his thirties, neatly dressed and solicitous. He promised to bring her lotion and other things she needed.

They said Billy Joe was doing fine, but Marge had to understand one thing. Voyles and Gonzalez didn't think they could represent the two of them simultaneously. Marge had to realize her interests were far different than her ex-husband's. She didn't want them to represent both of them anyway. If a crime had been committed, Billy Joe had to take responsibility, not her.

The attorneys told her the government wanted to talk to her, maybe arrange a deal. If she cooperated it would require separate attorneys. Tina had her own lawyer, and he planned to file an insanity defense, and in all likelihood Tina would become a government witness. If Marge cooperated as well, she might not get any prison time, or at least receive a reduced sentence.

Marge didn't know what to think. She prayed for guidance.

HAROLD Young and Harlan Rynard walked to the interrogation room for another session with Manuel Robinson.

The investigators had reason to be pleased. They had statements from a dozen witnesses, including a damning statement from Willard's former wife, and, if there was yet nothing to tie Willard directly into the shooting, they had everything but that. They now had a statement from a woman named Velma Caldwell, and she would testify that on the Wednesday night or Thursday morning when Mrs. Jackson was shot, she had been with Robinson, Willard and Pollitt, that there was a rifle in the car, that the men had dropped off the women and left in the middle of the night, and that the men had returned later to pick up Pollitt. Obviously from there they had gone to Annie Young's to split the money.

And there was Manuel, cool and stupid, wanting to outfox them when he didn't have to say anything, giving them tidbits of information when silence could be his ally. Of course Robinson wanted to point the finger at Willard, but why talk at all? Let him hang himself with his own statements, the detectives thought.

In his orange jumpsuit, the bald-headed prisoner greeted the two detectives and proceeded to tell the same story he offered up on the night of his arrest, but with variations. Billy Joe gave him the money to hold, he didn't know the source, and while he had been at Marjorie Jackson's place twice, he knew nothing about her murder.

"He didn't tell you where he got this money?" Young asked.

"No," Manuel said. "I'm not one to ask questions."

"Did you have any idea where he got this money?"

No, Manuel had very little curiosity. All he could remember was removing the money bands.

"Because you thought the bands that were on there could be traced?" Young pressed.

"No, no, not that. It's just that, you know, I was going to do all of them like that, but, you know, like I didn't know what bank or what, you know, I just...."

"But you knew where the money came from, in your own mind?"

"Let's just say I had a pretty good idea, but being definitely, no, I didn't."

Manuel was vague about the dates when he went to the Jackson house.

"Well, I believe the first time was at least....oh, it had to be at least two and a half weeks before the involvement...had to be that long."

"What happened when you went out there the first time, in the daytime?"

"Nothing."

"Did you drive by? Did you stop? Did you go in?"

"I didn't drive. I wasn't driving, because I don't know my way."

"You weren't driving? Well, what did you do? Stop there?"

"No, we just drove around, drove up. I remember he came out of this long road, we went down this other long road. We just went by the house, like I described to you, all these bushes, weeds, it looked real weird. Then we turned—think it's the street right next to the corner there—and we turned, and we went back and we went up."

On the second visit, at night, Billy Joe got out and stood by the car, Manuel said. He suggested the white man went up by the house while he drove around the block. Later, talking to Willard at the Shalimar, Willard told him he was afraid the woman who lived there might be a witch.

"That kind of tripped me out, because I, you know, well, he had a kind of serious look on his face, and it made me think he really believed in witches. And when he got to telling me what somebody had told him, evidently, you know, it had me thinking maybe this woman is a real voodoo somebody, something weird."

Robinson said Willard told him some guys he knew had a map of the house, and that two kids had robbed the woman.

"Did he ever make the statement that he was going to blow her away?"

"Not to me."

MARGE made up her mind.

With the counsel of her new attorney, she agreed to cooperate. They took her to the FBI office and sat her in a chair. FBI agents, two deputy prosecutors and an assistant U.S. attorney listened. She described everything she could recall. She gave two extensive statements, including things she was told about how and why Marjorie Jackson was murdered.

On a warm sunny summer day, they drove her from jail to a bridge over the river south of Mooresville. Here she pointed to the place where, she said, her ex-husband threw the rifle and toolboxes, all of which divers soon recovered. Then, in the company of FBI agents, a deputy marshal and the marshal's wife, she flew to Arizona.

North of Phoenix, in the desert, she pointed to a spot by a paloverde tree. "That's where the money is buried," she said.

She watched as agents dug up two cardboard boxes containing $1,673,460, one of them with the name MARGE printed on it.

10: F. LEE BAILEY

"Oh," the auctioneer was saying in a steady rain, "I think just about anybody would like to have the teeth. I wouldn't mind having them myself. Make a nice conversation piece. Gold inlaid false teeth, which I don't know how much they're worth. Somebody'll buy them just to say, 'Oh, these are Marjorie Jackson's chompers.'"

Several thousand people had gathered outside Earl's Auction Barn, their umbrellas offering a patchwork of color under an early summer rainstorm. A circus-type tent had been set up. Armed security people patrolled the perimeter. A sense of expectancy rippled through the gathering crowd. Photographers took pictures, TV crews moved through the muddy four-acre parking lot, and word went around that a network film crew had arrived. All newsmen were required to have special passes. Although it was not yet 10:30 in the morning, people munched Coney dogs and popcorn and sipped soda from iced tubs.

Under the umbrellas, in the rain tent, the people shared a feeling of intimacy. Some had paid extra for the privilege of being the first to peek into some of the green plastic garbage bags from the house. It was like examining someone's most intimate possessions while they were away from home.

As the eleven o'clock starting time neared, the crowd pressed forward. Like a carnival, one had a shot at a prize for a few coins. Marjorie Jackson, the murdered grocery store heiress who treated money like toilet paper. Who would be one of the lucky ones, to open a box or drawer and find a hidden fortune?

People came from a dozen states, mainly Indiana, Illinois, Kentucky and Michigan. The publicity about the murder, the bizarre millionairess and her strange treasure trove was a siren lure. All possessions had been removed from the house and stored for inventory. Earl Cornwell, a professional auctioneer with a silky twang, was retained to peddle Marjorie's earthly goods. Publicity about the sale included the news that a truckload of boxes and garbage bags would be up for sale. No one could miss the message that an overlooked necklace or handful of cash might lay undetected in a handkerchief or washcloth.

In death Marjorie had found friends and relatives around the country. People were lured by the thought there were no children, intrigued by reports of no will, or convinced of some genealogical line tracing to President Andrew Jackson. Actual claims against the estate numbered more than fifty, including distant relatives on both sides of the family. Dozens of other people wrote in hopes of receiving some portion of Marjorie's assets.

Letters came from virtually every state, from the piously sincere to the totally unbelievable. A man from Michigan wrote to assert a claim in behalf of Jesus Christ. A Californian who traced his roots to Andrew Jackson made claim with a note that he owned one of Old Hickory's dueling pistols.

Others wrote in behalf of their religions, asking for money in the belief that Marjorie would have wanted her fortune applied to some Christian pursuit. People sent charts of their family's histories. Others remembered communications with the deceased in which she had made known her intention to generously bequeath her money to them.

Even Howard Willard, from behind bars, had a claim. He wanted the Lincoln he had wrecked, reasoning that he took title to the car before anything happened to Marjorie Jackson.

The probable heir was Marjorie's half-sister, Roberta. She had the principal claim of blood. Once the house was sold and the furnishings auctioned, the pre-tax value of the estate was expected to be substantially in excess of $9,000,000.

Speaking into a microphone, Cornwell put the first item up for bid, a marble-top table.

"Do I hear ten dollars....do I hear ten....TEN DOLLARS....do I hear fifteen?"

There was a brief flurry before Cornwell closed at $30, a suburban mayor being the lucky bidder.

A stack of towels went for $11, another for $18. A woman bought several housecoats for $22.50. The bronze Cadillac Seville went for $12,000, to an attorney's wife who went home and received three dozen offers for the car within a few days. The other Cadillac went for $14,000, to a retired salesman. A stool sold for $5, a mailbox for $26, and three handfuls of parrot feathers went in lots of $10 each. A bank clerk bought two housecoats; a few days later, a woman called from North Carolina offering to buy them.

A cheap burglar alarm the size of a cigarette pack went for $22.50. It had never been used.

One woman scooped up more than $1,000 worth of goods for her own private Marjorie Jackson Garage Sale. She got perfume and cold creams, a trunk of new shoes, fifty sets of pajamas with only ten bottoms, furniture, one hundred dish towels—the list went on.

The drizzle continued. Bibles, books, sheet music went up for grabs. A sewing machine, oriental rugs, porch glider, charred pianos, silverware and china, mink coats, Marjorie's underwear....

"Going once....going twice....SOLD!"

Into the evening, then past midnight, Marjorie's most personal possessions were sold to the highest bidder. The two-day auction yielded $68,490 before expenses.

But they didn't get the false teeth.

These were withheld at the last minute because of a dentist's claim on the estate. They weren't Marjorie's teeth, anyway. They belonged to her mother, dead eight years. As the autopsy demonstrated, Marjorie had her own teeth.

At least this was one secret she could keep in the grave.

EXACTLY nine weeks after the discovery of Marjorie Jackson's corpse, the two middle-aged daughters of the Nazarene preacher stood ashen-faced in the U.S. courtroom in Indianapolis.

Her voice frogged with melancholy, Marge acknowledged guilt to the crime of interstate transportation of stolen money, while Robertina pleaded guilty as an accessory.

Why, the judge asked, did Marge decide to own up to her transgressions?

"I'm doing it because I prayed," Marge replied. "I'm going to spend my life in heaven even if it means going to prison and behind bars."

Truly she was ready to face the future, to tell the truth to the extent she knew it, and face the consequences. All her life she had been a law-abiding person. Now she had no choice except to try to hold her head high, admit the mistakes of the recent past, and gird herself for the future, placing herself under the stewardship of the Almighty.

Would anybody believe her? Would anybody believe she did what she did because of love?

Would anybody understand how much she feared the thought of losing that man, even when she knew in her heart that she was a party to murder? As someone remarked, if Billy Joe walked into the ocean and asked her to follow him to Europe, she wouldn't think twice before kicking off her shoes and rolling up her slacks.

And now, if she testified against her former husband, as surely she must, would anybody understand why? Not that she wanted to hurt the man—never that. It was just that, finally, she had to stop him from pulling her down with him.

Now, in a way, his life was in her hands. Her new attorney had sealed the deal with the government, and her own penalty depended on how much she cooperated with the FBI and the Marion County prosecutor.

Poor Billy Joe. The truth shall set you free. Or would it?

W HO killed Marjorie Jackson?

If prosecutors thought Willard and Robinson both were guilty of murder or conspiracy to murder, they still had to settle the question of who pulled the trigger.

Well, Willard had the rifle. Willard had made the statement that he "wouldn't mind blowing the bitch away." Willard had fled the city. But when Marge Pollitt agreed to be a witness for the prosecution, she blamed Robinson, and a hearsay witness, her sister Robertina, backed her up.

In her thirteen-page statement summarized by the FBI, Marge described first going to the house with

Wadsworth, the first burglary attempt, Willard's obsession with the woman, meeting Manuel Robinson, and her ex-husband showing up with the first mountain of cash.

During this period, WILLARD admitted on Monday morning, May 2, 1977, while she was working, WILLARD and ROBINSON went to the "witch's" house and hid in her yard. While the woman was in the back yard talking to some workmen, he and ROBINSON simply walked into the front door of her house and helped themselves to some of her money.

Marge also described picking up Velma, waiting at the woman's apartment, and Willard and Robinson returning with boxes of money.

At that time EMANUEL ROBINSON indicated that it was necessary for him to shoot the woman. WILLARD and ROBINSON then had a slight argument in which WILLARD told Robinson that he did not have to shoot her. ROBINSON stated that she had a gun and that she would have shot WILLARD had he not shot the woman. At that point, EMANUEL ROBINSON reached in the back seat and pulled out some money from one of the bags and told POLLITT that she was a millionaire. ROBINSON also told her that he shot this woman low and that she would not die.

Later, Marge said, Willard gave more details:

WILLARD kicked in the door of her house when she refused to open the door. He stated that the woman cursed at them and told him to leave. However, ROBINSON managed to sneak in the door while the woman was talking to Willard and when WILLARD turned around to leave he heard a gunshot. He then turned around and re-entered the woman's house and saw her falling to the floor. WILLARD told her that he heard the woman say, "Don't hurt me any more. Take what you want."

Around midnight Friday, May 6, Robinson and Annie Young came to her house. Willard, who was worried about fingerprints at the crime scene, took a gasoline can and left with Manuel.

WILLARD indicated to her that the gasoline can that they took from her house leaked and that they had problems finding a new can. WILLARD stated that they finally were able to get a two-gallon gasoline can and that he believed that this was not enough gasoline to destroy the house.

Nine days later, Marge had a second session with investigators to fill in gaps. Less than a week later, Robertina and her attorney sat down with many of the same investigators and answered questions for a nine-page summary prepared by the FBI. About the shooting, she quoted Willard almost word for word as her sister.

WILLARD told her that he asked the black man why he shot the woman, and the black man told him that he had to shoot her since she had a gun. WILLARD stated, however, that he did not see the woman with a gun at any time. POLLITT had told her that after the black man and WILLARD returned and the black man was dividing up the money, the black man laughed about shooting the woman.

Yet both statements focused on something that obviously interested the investigators as much as the murder—the suggestion that F. Lee Bailey, America's best-known lawyer, had instructed the fugitives to go into the Arizona desert and bury money stolen during a murder.

As Marge Pollitt told the story, Willard drove to Arizona because he wanted to get an attorney and Bailey supposedly was in trial in Phoenix. She said Willard had several meetings with Bailey, once with Henry Gonzalez present. Bailey, she remembered, told Robertina she should return home with Timmy immediately. And:

> During one of the discussions that WILLARD had with BAILEY, she overheard BAILEY telling WILLARD that he should divide the money into four or five portions and bury it so that if the police were able to get it out of anybody where one amount was buried, they would not get all of it. That's why Willard buried more than a million dollars, Marge said.

In fact, half of the second interview focused on Bailey.

> On the last occasion that they met with BAILEY at the motel room, BAILEY stated that if they had any of the money buried that he would advise them to dig this money up and bury it in four or five different places. He told them that they had more to fear with gangsters and hoodlums holding them up than the law and that he had been getting telephone calls from Honolulu and other places in the United States to locate WILLARD. He stated that when they buried this money that they should have the holes marked in some way and that if any

of the gangsters or hoodlums caught them, they would take them to one hole, but they would not lose all the money. BAILEY also told them on that occasion to play it cool until they received further instructions from him since they did not look anything like the photographs in the paper and that they would be safe. He told them that he would make arrangements eventually to have them brought back to Indianapolis.

Robertina was questioned extensively about Bailey as well.

HARRELL was asked whether she knew how much had been given to BAILEY or the other attorneys, and she stated that POLLITT had indicated to her that besides a $5,000 check, she had to give a power of attorney for $14,000 which POLLITT had in her savings account. POLLITT told her he indicated to her that before it was all over it would cost every bit of $1,000,000 for all three of them to be defended.

ATTORNEY Jim Voyles studied his new client with the careful attention that had helped Voyles build a growing reputation as one of the most skillful criminal defense lawyers in the state.

A smooth, fluid, olive-skinned man in his thirties, possessing a waistline expanding only a little slower than his law practice, Voyles prided himself on meticulous preparation, multi-dimensional strategy, and the ability to think fast on his feet, especially when a witness had trouble keeping his or her imagination separate from the facts.

Despite Howard Willard's jail coveralls, Voyles thought he looked like a nice little guy with a haircut straight out of the 1950s. More importantly, Voyles didn't think Willard was a murderer, or even capable of murder. No, Howard might be a burglar, and probably not a very good one, but he wasn't a killer, the lawyer concluded.

When Willard insisted he didn't shoot Mrs. Jackson, Voyles believed him. Possibly Willard was present when the woman was gunned down, but it could not have been planned, and if Willard could have prevented it he very likely would have. Despite likely testimony that Willard made boastful threats, Voyles felt reasonably certain that Howard's mouth, lubricated by alcohol, ran well ahead of his nerves. In fact, Willard had been complaining about the tranquilizers he had to take in jail just to keep his stomach settled.

Voyles pondered what to do about Marjorie Pollitt.

If she testified against her former husband, the thrust would be strong on the crimes of burglary and arson and yet somewhat favorable—maybe—on the crime of murder. The lawyer leafed through the statements Marjorie gave the FBI. The first was a chronological overview with a key statement, that Robinson said he had to shoot Mrs. Jackson because she had a gun. Well, no weapon had been found at the scene.

Robinson would be tried separately. Voyles didn't yet know what to make of the statements

Robinson supposedly had made to the sheriff's detectives. Clearly, though, Manuel didn't have enough brain power to singe a cotton ball. Or maybe the man possessed the kind of canny creativeness ex-cons often manifest.

Marge's second interview was rather spotty, an attempt to fill gaps, with considerable emphasis on her meetings with F. Lee Bailey. Voyles knew the FBI and prosecutor wanted to find out if Bailey had committed a crime, but he didn't expect anything to come of it. Henry Gonzalez, his co-counsel, had been called into the local grand jury, but Marion County had no jurisdiction in Arizona. Voyles doubted the feds had enough to take the issue any further.

While Willard didn't believe Pollitt would take the stand against him, Voyles knew better. The testimony would seal the state's case. Willard thought that if his former wife did testify, however, she would help his case, not hurt him. Voyles knew this would depend entirely on how a jury perceived her.

Willard at least was cooperative, not trying to play jailhouse lawyer. He appeared anxious to help Voyles and Gonzalez, and he listened carefully as Voyles outlined their initial strategy.

The federal case, interstate transportation of stolen money, was virtually airtight. One way or another, Howard would get federal prison time. The state's case was far more important, for the potential penalty was much more severe, even though Indiana, at the time, did not have the death penalty. Voyles wanted to suppress as much of the FBI evidence as possible, in hopes it couldn't be used in the state prosecution.

Now Voyles outlined the next step. The U.S. attorney's office had proposed a deal. If Willard would agree to a plea of no contest, the government would oppose the motion, though only for the record, and recommend an executed sentence. In this way the defense wouldn't have to lay out its strategy for the Marion County prosecutor to ponder before the murder trial.

Willard agreed. On Aug. 29, he changed his federal plea from not guilty to no contest.

NOT until November did Willard's trial get underway. People filed into the court wing of the City-County Building hoping to get a seat to see and hear the details of murder and scandal.

Now the state of Indiana would reveal some of the ghoulish things which heretofore could only be summarized in newspaper stories and TV reports. The prosecution spoke confidently of overwhelming evidence.

Steve Backer, a bright young attorney with courtroom presence, had assembled the state's case, but the prosecutor himself, Jim Kelley, joined him at the front table. Kelley well remembered his frustrating meeting with the murdered woman in this very building. He also knew that details about F. Lee

Bailey's unusual meetings with Willard and Pollitt would become public for the first time.

Behind the bench, handsome, graying John Wilson imposed a business-like but patrician presence. An experienced trial judge, Wilson was known for the wit of his colloquy with lawyers, and he did not oppose cameras, allowing closed circuit TV and videotaping of the proceedings, unusual for Indiana.

Voyles and Gonzalez huddled at the defense table. Gonzalez had a penchant for bright ties and jackets but carried the demeanor of a man who had won more than his share of courtroom trophies. Indeed, in his home state of Florida, he was known as one of the premier trial lawyers; his best-known client was Mafia boss Santo Trafficante.

To their right sat Willard, his face frozen in resolve. Facing sentencing in the federal case, he also seemed wearied by the death of his mother a month ago. For the trial he had his hair cut so the sideburns only crept halfway down his cheeks. He looked uncomfortable in his gray polyester suit with plain dark tie. The wisp of moustache had vanished.

Voyles and Gonzalez did not plan to put their client on the stand. Whatever the state's evidence, the fulcrum point would be Pollitt's testimony, and what would she say once she looked twenty feet or so across the room into Howard's dour face?

The defense hoped for acquittal on the murder charge; this was their best chance. If burglary, arson and conspiracy convictions were likely, they would work to exonerate Willard of homicide. After all, the chain of evidence should demonstrate that Robinson pulled the trigger without Willard's foreknowledge or approval. In this sense, Marge would be the best witness for the defense as well as the prosecution. If the jury liked her, they might feel the same sympathy for Willard. The defense would take the tack that Robinson used Willard.

Both sides were satisfied with the jurors. Of the twelve men and women the balance went to blue-collar—a laborer, mechanic, truck driver, printer, retired electrical foreman, grocery clerk. Predictably, the first witnesses laid out the mechanics of the crime. The state introduced a sketch of the house and grounds, and an aerial photograph. The deputy coroner gave his estimate as to when Mrs. Jackson died, and how. An arson investigator followed to describe the can of brake fluid and evidence it was used as an accelerant. Voyles and Gonzalez kept their questions routine, magnifying discrepancies where they could. At the end of the day Voyles objected because jurors were allowed to take notes.

The attorney started day two with another objection. The jury had seen Willard wearing handcuffs. The judge denied a motion for mistrial. A niece of the victim testified to establish that the murdered woman was a widow who lived alone. The pathologist described the autopsy, emphasizing that the decedent was dead before the fire. A police chemist described brake fluid found in burn samples. Voyles cross-examined him to get the admission that the original state of the fluid altered after combustion.

Harold Young took the stand, primarily to describe the condition of the master bedroom and the recovery of more than $5,000,000 from the closet. Another deputy traced the chain of custody of the bullet removed during the autopsy. A fingerprint expert proved to be of limited help for the prosecution. The next four witnesses were bank employees who traced the money and serial numbers given to Mrs. Jackson. All of this was a necessary prelude, for the third day began with someone who could place the defendant at Mrs. Jackson's house.

Until now, Voyles had been restrained, content to score small points. Now he was ready for Ralph Wadsworth II. The unctuous young hustler was a crucial link for the state because he not only could put Willard at the house on Spring Mill Road, he would put Marjorie Pollitt there as well.

Under Kelley's questioning the twenty-four year old witness came across as a nice young man, a city employee who had reluctantly, even inadvertently wandered into a criminal conspiracy. He recalled meeting Willard at L. Strauss, Willard's growing enthusiasm for booty, and the statement "I don't mind blowing the bitch away if she gives me any trouble." He described the second visit to the house, the unsuccessful attempt to break in, and Willard threatening to kill him if the police found out what they were planning.

Although nervous, Wadsworth made an effective witness. Voyles swiftly attacked his credibility, then turned to his testimony that he voluntarily went to the sheriff's department on May 9, two days after the discovery of the body.

"Okay, let's get this cleared up right now, Mr. Wadsworth. I'm going to hand you, for the purpose of refreshing your recollection, a document which is entitled the statement made by you. Would you look at the statement and see when that was made? Can you find it?"

"Yes." A constant tic pulled on his face.

"When is that?"

"It says 5-16-77."

"That would be May 16?"

"Yes."

"Swore to it under the penalties of perjury, didn't you?"

"Yes."

"That's not the ninth, is it? That's not immediately following the Jackson article in the paper, was it? It's the 16th of May, isn't it?"

"Yes, it is."

Sarcasm welled in the lawyer's voice. "And you talked about robbing L. Strauss, didn't you, with Jerry Hornick?"

"Jerry Hornick brought the subject up to me."

"And then you told him how much money they had there, didn't you? You guys discussed it, didn't you?"

Wadsworth acknowledged he had mentioned how much money the store had. He tried to duck when Voyles asked if he planned burglaries and robberies while working for the City Controller's office.

"You were talking about cracking the safe, weren't you?"

"Jerry Hornick said that—well, obviously the money is kept within a safe within an establishment like that, and Jerry Hornick said he knew a professional safecracker."

Voyles switched to the fact that Wadsworth had omitted from his original sheriff's statement other visits he made to the Jackson house.

"You were there with someone else to burglarize the home—Dick Schakel, Jerry Hornick and yourself, right?"

"No, I wasn't trying to burglarize the home."

"Were you sightseeing at it?"

"Obviously not."

Voyles was satisfied. While he couldn't prevent Wadsworth from drawing his client into a conspiracy, he had shown him as a lying conniver.

"Now," he concluded, "in January, when you were having all these discussions about burglarizing this home, you were also dealing with the police on potential job applications. Did you ever tell them about your conversations with Willard?"

"No."

"Nothing further," Voyles said.

There wasn't much he could do with the next witness, Willard's former wife, Osa. She came across as a simple, small town woman. She described how Willard had talked about wanting to rob a "weirdo" lady. In a sense, she was helpful to the defense, because she remembered Willard telling her that while he wanted to get a gun, he wouldn't have the guts to use it himself.

This was the beginning of the Mooresville testimony, a succession of witnesses describing how Willard and Pollitt deposited or spent stolen money. The final witness of the day was the salesman who sold Willard his dove gray Lincoln.

Tomorrow, the state's star witness would appear.

THE defense objected to testimony from Marjorie Pollitt. What she had to say represented confidential communications between husband and wife.

Young Steve Backer, who was enjoying his tactical duels with Voyles and his high-profile colleague from Florida, let a touch of exasperation rise in his voice. Any conversations between the defendant and Mrs. Pollitt were made in the presence of other parties, negating any potential marriage privilege. Judge Wilson agreed.

Marge wore a cream-colored pants suit set off by a polka-dot scarf. Her hair was frizzed and curled. Vanity kept her glasses tucked away in her purse. Her face looked pallid despite touches of makeup. She slouched nervously in the witness box, her voice at first a mere squeak in the microphone.

She avoided looking at the defendant. Only gradually did she calm herself. At the start each reference was to Mr. Willard. As the morning wore on, she began calling him by the name which had cemented their love.

Following Backer's methodical questions, she remembered meeting Hornick at the Little Eagle Tavern, meeting Wadsworth downtown, going to the Jackson house for the first time. Her words stumbling occasionally on ridges of grammar, she recalled going back to the house on the first burglary attempt, getting lost while driving around, meeting at the Complete Body Shop. Her words became a bridge between Willard and Robinson: meeting Manuel at the Shalimar, then how Mr. Willard had called her home from work to show her all that money from the witch's house.

Backer led her through buying the Lincoln, spending money, and going back to the Jackson house after Willard wrecked his new car. Then she described the events of the evening, from meeting Velma to going to Annie Young's apartment, the return of the two men, and splitting the money and leaving.

Referring to when she got into the car after Velma's, Backer asked, "Did you notice anything in the car that was not there when you were left off by Mr. Willard?"

"Yeah, some bags and stuff, whatever it was, in the back seat."

"And where did you sit, in the front or back?"

"Manuel slid over and I sat in the front."

"All right. Was there any conversation when you got in the car?"

"Yes."

"And what was that?"

"Well, Manuel said he had to shoot that woman, and Mr. Willard said, 'No, you didn't have to shoot that woman.'"

In a soft, matter-of-fact manner, Marge described getting rid of the rifle and toolboxes, Manuel and Billy Joe leaving to burn Mrs. Jackson's home two nights later, the flight from Indiana, and their odyssey in the West. It was effective testimony, apparently sincere and credible, with little to suggest coaching. Voyles scribbled notes, preparing to explore discrepancies between her testimony and earlier statements to the FBI.

Marge mentioned Willard had been contacting attorneys by telephone as they neared Flagstaff, Ariz.

"Did he ever tell you what attorney he was trying to contact?" Backer asked.

"Judge," Voyles interrupted, "may we approach the bench?"

Voyles informed Wilson that Marge was about to venture into the privileged area of a lawyer's relationship with a client.

"We'd object to that because that's irrelevant and tends to prejudice the jury," Voyles whispered.

The encounters took place outside the state of Indiana, after the murder, and not within the context of the state's charges. Privileged communications could be violated.

Backer disagreed.

"F. Lee Bailey told the defendant that his advice would be to go bury the money in the Arizona desert, and it may or may not come out from one of these gals that F. Lee Bailey went as far as to advise them to divide it up into various parcels and bury it in different locations so that if they had to lead somebody to the money, they'd still have money left over to find for themselves."

This was important, he said, because of scheduled testimony from FBI agents that Mrs. Pollitt did lead them to buried money, money stolen from Marjorie Jackson.

"Mr. Voyles has known this for months. He could call F. Lee Bailey if he wants to as a defense witness, if he wants to refute the fact that F. Lee told them to bury the money, but the fact remains that the money was buried, and it was buried after the conversation with F. Lee Bailey."

"Okay," Wilson said, "before you respond, I want to make sure that I understand the state's position. You are saying that it went beyond a mere attorney-client relationship, that Mr. Bailey, in fact, according to what you have just said, was in complicity as an accessory after the fact in substance to this case."

"That hurts me to say so about a fellow member of the bar, your honor," Backer said. "I'm afraid, based on the knowledge that I have, that is the testimony that will be....come from the witness stand today."

Voyles was adamant.

"Judge, if Mr. Backer wants to try Mr. Bailey, let him do it. But neither the United States attorney nor anybody else has seen fit to bring charges against Mr. Bailey. The FBI didn't even make a 302, an interview of him, that was ever furnished to us in this case."

Voyles insisted there was nothing to show Bailey had been the subject of any federal inquiry.

"Now, if Mr. Backer and Mr. Kelley want to take the position that Mr. Bailey may have committed a crime, well, they can bring him here in Indiana and Mr. Kelley can put him in front of the grand jury and ask him about it. But, clearly, your honor, they're putting up a big smoke screen to put his name, because he's a celebrated criminal attorney, in front of this jury for only one purpose, to prejudice the jury against the defendant."

Kelley interrupted to note acidly that there had been a notable interval between the time Bailey met the fugitives and when they were arrested. Anyway, he said, the state of Indiana had no criminal jurisdiction in Arizona.

"I don't see that this has the least bit of materiality here. I regret very much that Mr. Bailey's name has come up in this evidence, but if Mr. Bailey chose to give the advice which he apparently gave, I would say he involved himself."

Voyles proposed limiting Marge's testimony to the fact that money was buried. He wanted to put Willard on the stand about the meetings.

But the judge had heard enough. Any evidence of flight, concealment of the fruits of a crime, and aiding or counseling anyone who committed the crime was admissible. "Any evidence of the name of the person who aided after the fact would be admissible in evidence, no matter who it is."

Marge resumed her testimony, mentioning Bailey several times over Voyles's objections.

"And what," Backer asked, "did Mr. Bailey tell Mr. Willard, to the best of your recollection?"

"Told him a lot of people buried stuff out there on that desert, and if he had that money buried he should dig it up and put it in four or five parcels, because he was getting calls and there were mobs or gangsters and everything a'looking for us, and that they would get us, and not the law."

"All right. Why did….did he specifically state as to why to bury it in various places?"

"Yes, he said that if any of these mobs or gangsters or anything got ahold of us, that they would grab me and harm me in order to get Mr. Willard to tell them where the money was, and that he should know how much he had in each place, so that he could tell how much, you know, and where to get it."

"What did Mr. Willard do with the money when you were in Arizona?"

"We buried it."

Direct examination was nearly complete. Marge had been like a welder bolting down the state's case. The prosecution had only a few more questions.

"Why did you go on this trip with Mr. Willard?" Backer asked.

"Because I loved that man. Because all I seen was money, and I thought for the first time in my life that maybe I could live a little bit and help my kids and the rest of my family."

Backer sat down with obvious satisfaction.

Voyles wanted to be careful. There was no need to tear her apart. Marge had been damaging and helpful, putting Willard in the crime but naming Robinson as the triggerman. She seemed to have won over the jury, or at least enough of the jury to secure her credibility.

The attorney took her back through her story, filling in details, correcting misimpressions. He was willing to let her identify Willard as a burglar and perhaps arsonist, but not a murderer. Towards the end Voyles brought out a letter she had written to Willard's sister insisting Willard couldn't kill. The overall effect was of a simple woman who fell into a web of crime, perhaps with a whiff of greed but really out of blind love for a criminal, believe it or not.

By contrast, the next witness, Marge's sister Tina, appeared dazed and repentant, almost a victim herself. Recounting her conversations with Willard and her sister, Tina again pointed the blame for the shooting at Robinson.

The state returned to hard evidence. Deputies described the recovery of the rifle and ballistics tests to prove the fatal bullet could have been fired from it.

Again the defense magnified small variances and flaws.

The trial recessed for the weekend.

From his office in Boston, F. Lee Bailey issued a statement:

"I told him (Willard) I would represent him only if he would surrender and return the money. I told him that the county sheriff in Indiana had stated publicly that gangsters were looking for Willard and would kill him and his party to take the cash if they found him. I suggested for the safety of the child he place the money somewhere for safekeeping while I negotiated his surrender and not keep the money in the camper."

There the matter ended.

Monday morning, Voyles argued with the judge that the scheduled testimony of FBI agents should be disallowed on grounds that they illegally searched the Winnebago in Arizona. Overruled. A succession of agents came to the stand, closing with how Marjorie Pollitt took them to the desert where they dug up boxes containing $1,673,460.

A promising interruption came. The Indiana Supreme Court told Wilson to stop the videotaping of the trial. At that Wilson rejected a new defense motion for a mistrial.

More FBI agents testified, tracking the stolen money and putting the defendant's palm print on some of it. Annie Young came next. Her answers terse and vague, Robinson's girlfriend wasn't good on dates, but she described how Willard and Robinson counted the money that night in her apartment.

Velma Caldwell, Manuel's other girlfriend, followed. She helped the defense a little, for she could not identify Willard in the courtroom.

The state rested.

For Voyles the trial had gone pretty much as expected. While the judge had sent some flak his way, and, as always, he second-guessed his own cross-examinations, Voyles felt reasonably satisfied. The state, after all, had a pretty good case, considering other trials Voyles had contested. As clients go, Willard had done a fair job of leaving mud prints everywhere he wallowed.

Now, however, Voyles worried. For several days Howard had been lobbying to let him take the stand. Willard seemed consumed with a desire to testify, certain he could tell the story better than anyone else. Voyles smelled disaster. He thought they had a reasonable shot at acquittal for murder.

"Look, Mr. Voyles, I think I need to testify," Willard whispered once again.

"You can't testify, Howard. You can't do anything to hurt yourself."

"I think I just got to. I'll hurt my case if I don't."

Unable to dissuade him, Voyles had his secretary type up a letter recommending that Willard avoid the witness stand. He showed the letter to the judge in chambers. Wilson shrugged. The man had a right to testify, if he wanted to go against his attorney.

On Tuesday morning, Voyles recalled the arson investigator to straighten out a few matters. Then he turned to the bench.

"The defense calls Howard Willard, your honor."

Looking nervous, the defendant swore to tell the truth. Voyles elicited Willard's family history and part of his criminal background. Then:

"Between the week of May 2 and May 7 of 1977, will you tell the court and jury in your own words what happened?"

Willard cleared his throat.

"Well, May 2, early one morning, I and Emanuel Robinson drove up to Marjorie Jackson's house. Now, we just drove by. We drove up headed west the first time, and we noticed that she was in the yard talking to two men. We came by, driving real slow, and Robinson told me to stop, and this is directly north of her house. She had throwed some garbage bags over the fence. One of the bags had a hole in it, and there was some money sticking out of the hole, and this bag....in this bag we found $160,000. This woman had stuck money in bags all over the house and, accidentally, she had put trash in on this bag and threw it out."

Voyles was mortified. He couldn't look at the jurors. At the press table, some of the reporters covered their faces. In his cheap suit with brown hair tumbling over his forehead, Willard looked like a two-bit con man trying to sell cheap siding.

"We went to his house and we divided the money, $80,000 apiece. I went home. I called Marjorie and Marjorie left work and come home. She asked me where I got the money. I told her it came from the witch's house. I did not know Marjorie Jackson's name at the time. We just called her the witch. There was no burglary or conspiracy that day. If there had been a burglary she would have told the police. The police would have filed a report, a written report, investigated it, and it would have been filed with the court. She asked me where I got the money. I told her it came from the witch's house. She asked me if she was there. I said yes. She asked me if she seed me get the money. I said, told her, 'I don't think so, but if she did, she won't miss it,' which she didn't."

On the following Wednesday, he continued, he drove with Marge back to the Jackson house and checked the garbage bags, but there was no more money. They drove to the Shalimar and failed to find Robinson. Velma directed them to the Zodiac Club. Robinson wanted to go home and change clothes and discuss a business deal.

"So we dropped the girls off at a apartment and we went to the Shalimar Bar where we drank beer. Robinson asked me how much money I had left, and, well, from that eighty thousand I gave Marjorie about sixteen or seventeen thousand of it. I put three thousand in the savings. I think I put around seventeen thousand in the checking account. I spent money in the bar in Mooresville, and we paid off some bills, some smaller bills, and the rest I put in a safe deposit box."

Willard said Manuel was vague about the business proposition. Robinson proposed going to get some girls for a party, so he gave Manuel the keys to his car.

"He doesn't come back for two hours, or two hours and a half. When he does come back he's got the car full of bags and boxes, and he came in. I said, 'Where's the girls?' He said, 'Come on out here, I want, I got some things to tell you. I got something to show you.' He...and on the way to the car, he said he had burglarized Marjorie Jackson's home and got the money."

In other words, Howard wasn't even there.

Voyles rubbed his forehead. He felt sickened. It was the most incredible story he had ever heard. None of the jurors could look at Willard or his lawyers. Everyone seemed embarrassed.

Willard continued his monologue. They went to pick up Marge, and, afterwards, Robinson admitted he shot Mrs. Jackson. They went to Annie Young's and split the money.

"On the way down to the car—he walked us down to the car. He said, 'You better get rid of the rifle that's in your car.' I said, 'Why?' He said, 'Well, I shot the woman with it.' And then we got in another argument because I told him this rifle did not belong to me. It belonged to my wife, or Marjorie Pollitt, and that involved her. So we went home, and me and

Marjorie discussed this in the bedroom. First we didn't know what to do. We discussed about going to the police. We discussed about sending an ambulance to this woman's house. Marjorie said she couldn't get involved because her people would disown her, and I said, 'Well, the only thing to do is get rid of the rifle and hope everything comes out all right.'"

At the prosecution table Backer almost snorted at Willard's pathetic tale of gallantly wanting to protect Pollitt. Backer and Kelley sat spellbound. It was as if Willard was locking the cell door himself, as if he wanted to give them his testimony to secure the conviction even when they didn't need it.

According to Willard, he couldn't sleep thinking about the woman, so he drove in the darkness back to Marjorie Jackson's house. Marjorie wasn't there, and he went to Robinson's place, where Robinson described in detail how he shot the woman.

"I went home—no, I asked him again about this rifle. I said, 'How did you use the rifle when it wasn't loaded?' There was no bullets in the gun or the car. He said that he went to his mother's house and got shells for it, and then went directly out there. Now, Marjorie Pollitt testified that, to things here in court concerning this, what she...what she...I never told her...."

The judge overruled an objection. Willard resumed his soliloquy.

He remembered Robinson and Annie Young coming to Mooresville that Friday night, and leaving with Robinson, but not for the purpose of burning the house. They went to the Shalimar, picked up some girls, drove around for awhile, and he fell asleep in the car. When he awoke, Robinson was talking about getting rid of his fingerprints in the Jackson house.

"I said, 'Well, you'll have a hard time doing that.' We got home and parked, and we was walking up to the door. He said, 'Well, I've got a can in my trunk. I could go up there and set the house on fire and smoke the place up. They wouldn't find any fingerprints that way.' And I said, 'No, I don't believe you should do that because if this woman has went to the hospital' —because she was gone when I was, or I thought she was gone, I didn't see her—'she's told the police, and you wouldn't get within fifty feet of the house,' and he says, 'Maybe you're right.'"

Willard admitted Robinson gave Marge $30,000. He said Manuel seemed in a hurry to leave, and did so. Only on the radio the next morning did he learn of the fire. By then it had gotten too deep, so he fled the city with Marge. He had no idea he was wanted for any crime until he stopped in New Mexico and telephoned his sister in Indianapolis.

Suddenly Willard was finished. Kelley realized he could spend the remainder of the day riddling, if not ridiculing, Willard's testimony.

"Just one question, Mr. Willard."

"Yes?"

"What did you do with the other million dollars you got out of Marjorie Jackson's house?"

"What other million? Every penny that we had has been confiscated."

"That's your story," Kelly said sarcastically.

"That's true."

"That's all," the prosecutor said.

Final arguments were anticlimactic. The jury deliberated five hours before finding Willard guilty of murder and seven other charges, and recommending life in prison. Wilson formally pronounced the sentence just before Christmas. The life term would begin when Willard's federal sentence ended. The federal sentence was five years for conspiracy and ten years for transporting stolen money across state lines.

In federal court two weeks later, Marge was sentenced to five years in prison, Tina to two and a half years.

11: THE ROUND-UP

AT approximately 2:45 in the morning on Nov. 29, 1977, a week before the jury convicted Willard, a twenty-year-old exotic dancer stepped into the night after working her shift at the Naughty Lady Lounge on the east side of Indianapolis.

As she told police later, she was driving down the snowy street when a car forced her to the side of the road. Two men who had been in the nightclub got into her car. She knew one as Wally Bergin, Jr., an acquaintance from high school. Bergin called the other man Doug. Doug told her he was going to rape her. Wally explained that they were celebrating Doug's birthday.

The woman said Doug forced her to perform oral sex and then raped her. They released her after she promised Bergin she wouldn't tell anyone what happened.

On Dec. 21, police obtained warrants charging Doug Green and Wally Bergin with confinement, criminal deviant conduct, and rape.

Ironically, one of the investigating detectives was Marjorie Jackson's nephew.

ON the same day Green and Bergin were arrested, Jim Voyles answered the telephone in his office.

The caller identified himself as Gary Perkins, and Voyles began jotting notes. The lawyer realized this was the same man who had telephoned twice before with offers to testify for Willard in exchange for money. Now Perkins said he thought as much as $4,500,000 of Marjorie Jackson's money remained in the hands of thieves; he personally had seen $800,000.

Voyles told Perkins he might be able to earn something from the Jackson estate if he helped the executors recover any money. When Perkins hung up, Voyles called the U.S. attorney's office.

The matter might have ended there, except Voyles mentioned the call to Indianapolis Star reporter Joe Gelarden a few days later. There had been considerable speculation that some Jackson money remained missing. The fact was, attention focused on the circumstances of the murder. Except for the transitional roles of Hornick and Wadsworth, the year-old burglary of more than $800,000 had been forgotten. Once the murder dragnet went out, what happened before became a footnote.

Sheriff Gilman summoned Harold Young and Detective Sgt. Dave Paschall to his office.

"Take this thing and check it out," he ordered. "I want to know who's got that money and where it is."

New to the Jackson case, the tall, balding, bespectacled Paschall thought the man who called Voyles probably was a crank. Young suspected otherwise. Nearly a year ago, Perkins had provided limited information to Tommy Thompson, and that information focused on the allegation that Green and Bergin robbed Mrs. Jackson long before Willard and Robinson came sniffing around. The prosecutor's office had been unable to develop a case, largely because of the non-cooperation of the victim.

Now, she was dead. It was time to reopen the past.

Young and Paschall decided to start with Gary Walters. Although Tommy Thompson questioned how much Walters told compared to what he knew, Walters had been a friend of the principals. When Walters agreed to come downtown to answer questions, Thompson sat in on the interview.

The two greeted each other coolly. Since the Jackson murder, Walters had let it be known that he had warned the prosecutor's office six months before the murder that Marjorie Jackson was in jeopardy.

Now Walters said he had run across Bergin a few weeks ago. Wally had been living in Louisville but visited Indianapolis for the night life. In fact, Walters thought Bergin and Green had been arrested, for raping a go-go girl.

Young made no comment, but in his quiet way he was excited. A man in jail sometimes is willing to talk where a man comforted by his freedom will not.

Walters repeated what he had heard about the initial burglary, about Green and his wife being robbed, about the Greens buying a farm. Doug's wife had split from him because of the rape arrest, Walters thought, but Donna herself had fallen on hard times and was living on welfare.

"Donna knows a lot. I mean, that girl was there. You know, there's a hundred percent, it's not hearsay. That girl knows."

"Did you see the money at Bergin's house when it was supposedly burned by Bergin senior?" Thompson asked.

"I seen several thousand dollars of it. I've also seen Mr. Bergin....we went to a bank and Mr. Bergin took tens, fifties and twenties out of his pocket."

"How much did you see in Mexico?"

"Well, he (Wally) had about maybe somewhere between ten, twelve and thirteen thousand in $100 bills, brand new, in his pocket."

The young man answered questions for close to an hour. He volunteered that yet another employee of the Complete Body Shop might have visited the Jackson home.

"Okay," Thompson said, "but you don't know anything other than that about any other burglaries at the Jackson home?"

"No," Walters said.

The detectives returned to their office and heard some encouraging news. Green and Bergin in fact had been arrested on a rape complaint. The incident had occurred on Nov. 29, Green's birthday. Bergin had made bond. Green remained in jail.

IN his cell in the Marion County Jail, Doug Green brooded.

"I just don't have that kind of money to get you out," his mother had written to him. "I'm sorry I don't. I know it is very hard for you to stay there when you are innocent but I don't know what to do about it." Mrs. Green had made some Christmas fudge which the jailers refused to deliver. She and her husband had given Doug's sister money to buy food for her and Randy's baby, but they couldn't afford much more. They gave Judy $10 to pass along to Doug for candy and cigarettes.

"Well, Doug," she ended her letter, "about all I can do is hope and pray that everything will be OK and you will be out before long and a free man. Trust in God and be truthful and I am sure He will help you through this difficult time in your life. Just remember, Dad and I and everybody loves you."

Doug was bitter and angry, at being unable to make bond, but also because he thought Donna was having a good time while he rotted in jail. He had started to believe Donna didn't need him any more. She was just a kid, the mother of his lovely daughter

Christie. It was, he thought, savagely ironic. Not so long ago he had been rich and happy go lucky. Now he was broke, in jail, friendless, facing a bleak future, and worried about his wife and daughter.

And Judy, who had spent $100 bills like she printed them herself, Judy was broke too, working as a grocery store checker. The money seemed to have changed all their lives for the worse.

Doug scribbled on a piece of paper. He wanted to write his most intimate thoughts, his philosophy of life, his manifesto for the people in the world who seemed bent on hurting each other. Most of all he wanted to paint the rage and frustration aching in his bones. If he did not get out of jail soon, he thought he might try to kill himself.

He stopped scribbling and began to write to Donna. The words came in short, powerful bursts. Donna, Christie, Christie, Donna. If he lost Donna he would never lose Christie; he could never lose his daughter.

When he finished he added a postscript. He told his wife he knew she was living with another man.

"You lied, you cheated, you deserted me when I needed you the most. I suffered physically and mentally because of you. You destroyed me in many ways, Donna. I suffered in this jail because I thought you were true to me. I thought I could trust you beyond a doubt. Don't ever try to convince me to go back with you. You and other people are going to suffer worse than I did and have been. I promise you that. VENGENCE IS MINE."

Early one afternoon, the deputy came to the cellblock and informed Green he was wanted in the Detective Division.

The brown-uniformed officer said little as they rode the elevator downstairs. A huge metal door clanked open. Another barred door opened at the rear of the detective offices. A man signaled him into an interrogation room. Young and Paschall waited.

"I got nothing to say," Green told them.

Paschall had a speech prepared. It was the standard detective's speech, with variations. The thrust was to convince the suspect it was better for everyone and especially himself to talk. To the layman these overtures might seem transparent. To a person in jail, especially one without much legal experience, they can be compelling. Someone with limited options is vulnerable to persuasion.

Paschall did not hurry. He explained they were not so much interested in the rape case as the burglary at the Jackson home seventeen months earlier. Paschall didn't mask the fact that he and Young knew a lot about Wally and Jerry and Gary. He noted that a grand jury would hear testimony, and additional criminal charges probably would be filed.

The detectives weren't certain what clicked. It may have been when Paschall mentioned they undoubtedly would arrest Green's wife and he might lose custody of his daughter.

"Okay," Green said, "I'll tell you about it. What do you want to know?"

To Tommy Thompson, listening to the former maintenance man bare his soul was like having an old, foggy negative developed into a clear, detailed photograph.

Green's story sounded like a bar-room yarn, two punk kids snatching an estimated $820,000 in a burglary. But the money had poisoned Green and his family, ultimately bringing impoverishment rather than enrichment. Doug was a troubled young man, indeed.

Green gave a lengthy statement and passed a lie-detector test.

Next Paschall and Young brought in Donna Green. At eighteen, with a bawling daughter in tow, she had the look of a minor flower that would never regain its bloom. Grandfather Harold Young took her aside to explain that the burglary investigation had been reopened; they did not believe she was a party to the crime, only that she had knowledge of and received some of the stolen money. If she told the truth she would not be arrested.

"Okay," Donna agreed.

Among other things the woman's statement provided a witness, other than Doug Green, that Walter Bergin, Jr., had possessed stolen money. The detectives believed her when she said she never knew precisely what Doug's share was.

Paschall asked her about Doug's sister, Judy Parrish. Donna said she had talked to Judy earlier in the day.

"And did she say anything about the money today?"

"Yes, she told me that we were all gonna get arrested, and I asked why, and she said, 'I don't know, I just think we are.'"

Paschall wondered if Gary Walters ever said anything about breaking into the Jackson house himself, as Doug suggested. Donna thought he did.

"What did he have to say about that?"

"That him and Wally had gone back to Mrs. J's house."

Next, Green's brother Danny gave a voluntary statement, conceding that he, too, had received stolen money.

The following day the two detectives obtained warrants charging Wally Bergin with burglary and conspiracy. He arranged to surrender, and bond was set at $1,000,000. Skulking at his second arrest within two months, Wally made it clear he had no interest in talking to detectives.

Judy Parrish did. The statement Green's sister provided was a carefully layered cake of truth and half-truth, pointing the finger away from herself as much as possible. But she could not deny that she possessed stolen money, fought with her brother, and failed to go to the police. Adamantly she denied arranging for Doug and Donna to be robbed in their apartment by men who threatened to murder them.

Her husband, Randy Parrish, was the next to talk. He gave the investigators the keys to a new car he and Judy had purchased with Jackson money, and, a few days later, surrendered a truckload of household goods.

Young and Paschall were pleased. Once Green talked, everything started falling into place. They expected to make eight or nine arrests, and they stood to recover a substantial amount of property purchased with stolen money.

Still, they talked about Wally and his father. Mr. Bergin made an inviting target. He was the only true adult in the whole mess. If the retired railroader had cooperated, Mrs. Jackson might still be alive. Instead he had lied to the grand jury.

Two days after Wally Bergin, Jr.'s arrest, his attorney worked out a deal with the prosecutor's office. His client would plead guilty to conspiracy, the burglary charge would be dropped, and his bond reduced. In return Wally would tell all, take a lie detector test, and testify whenever necessary, except, if it came down to that, against his father.

Unlike Green, young Bergin was sullen, tense and reluctant. To the detectives he had the look of a spoiled kid angry the world owed him less than he thought.

Yes, he broke into Mrs. Jackson's residence. Yes, he gave Hornick part of the loot. Yes, he gave Gary Perkins $10,000 and told him where it came from. Yes, he tried to break into the Jackson house a second time, unsuccessfully, with Gary Walters. Furthermore, his father took at least $200,000 from his car. Recently, Wally had dug up a $50,000 cache from his father's backyard in Louisville and taken one or two thousand dollars.

"Do you think your Dad will dig up this money and move it some place else?" Paschall wondered.

"I couldn't say."

"Let me ask you this. Do you think your Dad would be just as happy to surrender the money and get as much off his back too?"

"I don't know. I don't know."

The revelation of money buried in the yard in Louisville was the hottest lead to develop so far. Although Wally confirmed his father committed a crime, he wouldn't have to testify. But the detectives wanted him to telephone Mr. Bergin. If the man knew his son had been arrested, it might cause him to make a wrong move.

With the consent of Wally's attorney, the call was placed. Wally started crying on the phone.

"Dad....I've been arrested."

Hesitating, Walter Bergin, Sr., asked why.

"For all this money."

"What money?"

"The Jackson money. I told them everything, and I told them you've got part of the money."

"Well, why would you tell them something like that?"

"I've got to get all of this off my mind," Wally sobbed.

While Wally's attorney took the phone, Paschall went to another phone to ask the Louisville office of the FBI to begin surveillance of the Bergin residence.

The prosecutor's office obtained a warrant charging Mr. Bergin with perjury. From Louisville, Bergin retained an attorney and arranged to surrender under $500,000 bond.

His hair graying, his thin face weary, wearing a sweater with his collar out campus-style, Bergin arrived in Indianapolis to be placed in custody, and shook his head.

"I don't know anything," he said. "I don't know what you're talking about. I told the truth to the grand jury."

Soon Bergin would know that even his daughter was in custody; Young and Paschall obtained a warrant charging Maywin Jackson with theft, based on Wally's admission that he gave her $5,000.

Unexpectedly, the investigation turned back to Gary Walters.

Donna Green telephoned to say that Walters had called asking her to forget he had ever bragged about going to the Jackson home and trying to break in with Wally. The detectives consulted with Thompson.

Thompson didn't think they had enough evidence to get a conviction against Walters. The foremost problem was the lack of a date. Wally couldn't remember when they went back to the house, other than a few months after he and Doug scored. The law required criminal charges to be specific, especially as to the date of the crime. Because nothing was taken, there could be no fruit of the crime, and no physical evidence. Besides, Wally was reluctant to testify against Gary.

Young and Paschall contented themselves with arranging arrest warrants for Randy and Judy Parrish. Meantime, they waited for the prosecutor to decide whether to get warrants to allow them to cross state lines and dig up the yard around the Bergins' Louisville home.

IN jail, several things troubled Walter Bergin, Sr.

His son and daughter had been arrested. In effect, his son had turned him in. What about his wife—would the sheriff's men come after her as well? What would happen next? Bad luck had cursed the family ever since he looked inside Wally's trunk.

His cellmates bothered Bergin too. Another jail resident was Emanuel Robinson, the man accused of murdering Marjorie Jackson. What if Robinson or one of his cutthroat friends got the idea they could force him to talk about the money? All of these people had friends on the outside. Money did crazy things to people, and some of these people were crazy anyway.

In another part of the building, Paschall stayed behind to talk to Wally after Young had gone home after a long day. In the clammy interrogation room, Paschall chatted with the youth about the futility of his father's situation. If Mr. Bergin changed his mind and decided to cooperate, it might work in his favor when he went to court.

Wally got the message. "Can I talk to my Dad?"

"Sure."

"I think I can get him to talk to you. Can I talk to him down here?"

"No problem."

When Mr. Bergin arrived, wearing the same kind of jail coveralls as his son, the older man appeared wary.

"Sit down, Mr. Bergin," Paschall commanded. "I'm going to talk and you're going to listen."

Paschall discussed Wally's confession, the other statements now on file. It appeared Bergin's wife would be charged with conspiracy. The whole family would be in jail. Why? Over stolen money that had only caused trouble from the moment the Bergin clan took possession. How long would it go on? Did Bergin want to see his family destroyed?

Bergin shook his head. The publicity had ruined them already, he said hoarsely.

"I want to give the money back. I wanted to give it back right away, when this thing came up, but I didn't think I could trust Young or Thompson. I think I can trust you, Paschall."

He looked at his son. "Why would you tell on me? I was trying to do the right thing for you. I was afraid you'd get killed."

Bergin hung his head. Wally looked like he might cry.

"Look," Paschall said, "I can talk to the prosecutor and see if they'll give you a suspended sentence."

"All right," Mr. Bergin agreed.

Paschall notified Young and his superiors before calling Thompson and Bergin's attorney. The lawyers argued heatedly over a suspended sentence, and Thompson finally relented. Considering Bergin's otherwise clean record, he probably would get a suspended sentence anyway. The agreement was put in writing. Bergin wanted his daughter freed, and Thompson agreed.

On a snowy day in February 1978, Bergin joined the detectives and attorneys on a small plane for a flight to the tiny airport in Bowling Green, Kentucky. Bergin's wife was to meet them, but when the plane taxied to a halt near two small buildings she was nowhere in sight. Only after an hour of waiting did she prove to be waiting herself at the wrong building.

Bergin kissed his wife and she led him to a station wagon. Opening the trunk, just as her husband had opened the trunk of his son's car on that fateful day more than a year ago, she removed a heavy plastic bag and handed it to Bergin.

They kissed again.

"Well, here it is," Bergin said as he handed the bag to the attorneys.

On the plane, they counted $236,900 in $100 bills.

T HE next target was Gary Perkins.

If Perkins had started the new investigation with his call to Voyles, it had to lead right back to him. Various confessions demonstrated something Perkins had failed to mention: Wally gave him $8,000 or $10,000 in stolen money to launder.

By arrangement Perkins agreed to surrender on a theft warrant. The twenty-five year old husband of Wally's former girlfriend flew in from his home in Cleveland, and admitted he, too, had received Jackson money.

The detectives turned to Jerry Hornick.

Although Hornick had testified before the grand jury more than a year ago, clearly he had violated the terms of the immunity conferred at the time. And Hornick was the source of everything. Hornick was the first to stalk the house. Hornick brought Wally in. Hornick received $10,000 from Green and Bergin. Hornick introduced Willard to Wadsworth. Hornick accompanied Wadsworth and Willard on their first break-in mission. And Hornick had lied.

For all of this it might be difficult to prosecute the man. The evidence consisted primarily of statements of two burglars, and how would a jury weigh the fact that Hornick at one point cooperated with the state?

Paschall and Young formulated a plan, and Thompson concurred. If Hornick agreed to plead guilty to theft and testify whenever necessary, they would recommend a suspended sentence. At this late date it wasn't a bad proposition. Hornick had moved back to his native West Virginia; extradition could be a problem.

Hornick's attorney listened to the proposal and arranged for Hornick to surrender, the tenth person to face charges in connection with the 1976 burglary.

Young and Paschall wondered how much jewelry Doug Green had tossed into the water company canal as he and Wally fled from the Jackson home that long-ago Sunday.

On a freezing March day, a team of six divers set a grid of some two hundred yards and entered the icy water. Visibility was zero, and a half-foot of mud and silt covered the bottom. After thirty-five unproductive minutes, the divers gave up.

Like some forgotten treasure, Marjorie Jackson's jewelry would remain hidden under the water.

12: MANUEL

Eൺ morning, Marge rested for a few moments and listened to the sounds of the other women stirring in their cells. Sleepy voices called out, metal clanged, toilets flushed. Through bars or screens the city outside did not change: buildings like dull paintings, a parking lot filled with cars, a railroad overpass which at least sent out the steady rumble of passing freight trains.

Marge always said her prayers, and these were treasured moments before the monotonous daily routine. She read and reread her letters, from Billy Joe or his family, from her daughters, from friends. Best of all she enjoyed the letters from the federal prison in Terre Haute. Billy Joe's last letter said:

"Hi honey. Just got off work and thought I'd drop you a fue lines. I phoned Mr. Voyles today and he said he was doing all he could to help me, then I phoned Henry Gonzalez, he was in Miami office. Henry said I had a rough case. He said they wouldn't have found me guilty of murder if you hadn't testified against me. Honey, I never hirt anyone in my life. I know that I took things from people, but what the hell, who hasn't at one time or other has stole something. But I'm not guilty of killing that woman. Why for did you get me all this time for? Honey, Henry said that I would never get out again, said I would die in here. Honey, how could you be so mean to take away the life of your loved one? I just can't understand and I'm upset now that I can't think straight. I got a letter from Roberson today he said that no one was going to testify against him he said his attorney would win his case and he will go free. Honey he killed that woman and he gets to go free and I will have to do the time for what he did. It just don't make sense."

What did make sense, Marge wondered. Billy Joe was in Terre Haute, she was in the county jail waiting for Robinson's trial, and their lives had been pulled apart like a sweater unraveled down to the last thread. What was the sense of anything?

She knew Billy Joe had filed a petition for reduction of his federal sentence. He also had requested a transcript of the federal proceedings preparatory to an appeal on grounds that his attorneys had coerced him into the no contest plea. But he was grabbing at straws, she thought. His letters reflected an obsession that some court would change his future. What about her? Did his obsession blind him to her plight? Even as he pledged his continuing love, never did he lament the empty future he had imposed in her life through his own failings.

In a few days she would have to testify in Robinson's trial. Billy Joe felt like he was a victim of

Robinson. He claimed Manuel had killed Marjorie Jackson and Billy Joe Willard was a victim too.

He expected Manuel to testify in his own behalf, and he was convinced Manuel's testimony would mean his own freedom.

ANYONE who expected Robinson's trial to be a choreographed replay of the Willard prosecution did not reckon on Manuel's attorney Arnie Baratz.

A sharp bantam of a man, in his early thirties, widely respected as a public defender, Baratz had his own ideas on how to defend against the state's tidal wave of evidence, and the cornerstone was that Marjorie Pollitt lied.

Baratz decided to turn the state's biggest gun the other way. And there would be no repeat of Willard's pathetic monologue which seemed to have so sweetly sealed his fate. Robinson would never say a word; Baratz would be his voice.

Because the trial had the promise of anticlimax, two young prosecution assistants, John Schwartz and Aaron Haith, drew the assignment. Haith had a personal attachment to the case. Two years ago, as a prosecutor's assistant, he had helped keep the Jackson house under surveillance during her bank withdrawals. Later he accompanied Thompson and the sheriff's men on their icy confrontation with Mrs. Jackson in her yard. Haith was not much older than Robinson, and, like the defendant, was black. The irony did not escape him. A black prosecutor was after the hide of a black man for killing a white woman with a noted hatred of blacks.

The state planned to call about forty witnesses. Marge Pollitt probably was the most important. This time her sister wouldn't testify; Robertina never met Robinson, and unlike the Willard case, any statements made to her about Robinson's crimes were hearsay. Johnny Williams would fill in some of the gaps.

The jury was seated, and a succession of detectives, firemen and arson experts paraded to the stand. Baratz hammered at discrepancies. Who first entered the house on the morning of May 7, 1977? If there was no evidence of forced entry, there was, technically speaking, no burglary. Baratz scored points.

Detective Sgt. Harlan Rynard was the first critical witness. Rynard told the jury about Robinson's voluntary admissions after his arrest.

"He stated that a man, a white man, had dropped this money off for him to keep for him, and then, later on, through conversation, the money was supposed to have been found behind a drugstore where the white man's wife had worked, and she took the money in a sack behind the store and left it for them."

Robinson admitted he had been at the Jackson house, that "he had been out to the house on two different occasions with Mr. Willard....he stated that Willard had gone in; he didn't go in."

Baratz probed a little. Robinson's statements were tape-recorded, were they not?

Yes.

And the taped statement was reduced to writing?

Yes.

Rynard said the transcript had been given to the prosecutor's office and mislaid. And the original tape also was lost, apparently by a secretary at the sheriff's office. But other tapes weren't lost, Baratz noted, only the tape of the principal suspect.

"Okay, did the secretary give it back to you or Sgt. Young after it was done?"

Rynard said he had no idea what happened to the tape. "The tape was either lost or we went ahead and taped other statements over the original tape."

"You mean the tape might have been erased?"

"That's right."

"Did you attempt to find out who it was who had the tape, which secretary?"

"Yes, we did."

"And do you know the name of that person?"

"No, I do not."

"It wasn't Rosemary Woods, was it?" (A reference to President Nixon's secretary).

But Baratz had not quite made his point.

"Now, at the time you had him in custody on May 9, 1977, at that point did you know the name Howard Willard?"

"Yes," said Rynard, "I had heard the name Willard."

"Willard—did you know the name Howard Willard?"

"No, I did not."

"Did you know the name Marjorie Pollitt?"

"Prior to talking to Mr. Robinson?"

"Yes."

"No, I did not."

On recross, Schwartz and Haith tried to repair the damage, but Baratz fired back. The fact was, Robinson gave the sheriff's men the names of Willard and Pollitt, even supplied Pollitt's phone number.

"Is that how you discovered that Marjorie Pollitt and Howard Willard were involved in this?"

"Yes," Rynard said.

Velma Caldwell helped shore things up. She testified about the events of that Thursday night, putting Willard and Pollitt at the Zodiac Club, with Robinson, and at her apartment.

Marge came next. She looked pale but not as nervous as her first appearance. Patiently she went through her story. Baratz was ready for cross-examination. Manuel and Billy Joe. Manuel, the black man she didn't like, Billy Joe, the white man she loved.

"Why did you go with Mr. Willard when he left town?"

"Because I loved him and wanted to be with him."

"Did you realize you were involved in very serious crimes?"

"No, I didn't have enough sense to know it would involve me just to be with him after he had done it and all, he had the money and all. I should have knowed better. I should have turned him in, but I didn't. That was a big mistake. I know that now."

Baratz referred to the night Marge acted as chauffeur for Willard, Wadsworth and Hornick in their first attempt to rob Mrs. Jackson.

"Why did you agree to drive those three people over to the house that night?"

"Probably because I had been drinking a few drinks, and, just like some stupid fool, because I loved my husband and just hung right in there by him."

"You loved Mr. Willard?"

"Yeah, I loved Mr. Willard."

"Still love him?"

"I'm trying to get over it."

Baratz perhaps was as satisfied as he could hope. The perception of the jury had to be different than when Willard sat on trial. Before, the jury could believe Marge told the truth despite her reluctance to hurt the man she loved. Here the jury might think she wasn't telling the truth, or at least all of it, because of the man she loved.

Next came Annie Young's neighbor, Annie herself, John Williams, others to put Robinson in possession of Jackson money. A dozen more witnesses followed. The defense called four prosecution witnesses before resting. Manuel did not testify.

Summing up, Haith and Schwartz emphasized the mass of the state's evidence. It was not necessary, Haith noted, for the state to prove who pulled the trigger, only that Robinson and Willard committed the burglary and Marjorie Jackson was killed during the crime. And, Schwartz amplified, the issue wasn't whether Robinson did some incredibly stupid things while in possession of stolen money after arson and murder; the issue was homicide, not brains.

Baratz had other notions. The case, he told the jurors, boiled down to one thing. Marge Pollitt's lies.

"Everything Marjorie Pollitt says about Manuel Robinson could have been done by Howard Willard. Willard and Pollitt were the only two people in the world who would say Manuel Robinson shot Mrs. Jackson, yet on the day he was arrested, he gave the names and telephone numbers of these people to the authorities. Why would he do that if he shot that woman?"

Baratz asked the jury to take note that Marge did not give the FBI a statement until early July, two months after the murder. "They gave her statements of other witnesses, and she made her testimony fit." While Willard and Pollitt were fleeing the state, Robinson remained in Indianapolis. Why? "I don't think Manuel Robinson knew anybody was killed. He was too busy spending money."

The jurors deliberated seven and a half hours. Manuel sat impassively when they returned.

Guilty, two counts of first-degree burglary, two counts of conspiracy to commit burglary, guilty of arson and guilty of conspiracy to commit arson. Not guilty of armed robbery. Not guilty of murder.

The judge sentenced him to ten to twenty years in prison.

MARJORIE Pollitt didn't often think of Marjorie Jackson.

But sometimes at night she had nightmares in which the other Marjorie might have been a participant. There was a memory of that crazy house and the woman yelling to be left alone with her privacy and her money. When she had bad thoughts, Marge turned to the Bible, to God. She came to realize how far she had strayed, and in this realization was the certainty that, in spite of everything, God was watching over her. In all her wandering she had strayed from the one thing which forever promised redemption and salvation. The wonderful thing was, once she came back into the embrace of Jesus Christ, it was as though she had never strayed.

The State of Indiana had dismissed all charges against her. Altogether then she spent eleven months in jail and eight months in prison, in West Virginia, before she was released on federal parole. When she returned to Indiana she found her family waiting, ready to accept her back into their lives. For a time she worked in a motel. She did not return to Mooresville at first, for she feared the Ku Klux Klan might try to retaliate because she brought black people to her house.

She got a job in a factory, and when someone asked her if she really was the woman who had been involved in the Jackson case, she denied knowing anything about it.

She found an apartment and wrote to Billy Joe and received his letters in return. He had pretty much exhausted his appeals, but he didn't plan to give up. In prison, he knitted a sweater and sent it to her. He made her a beautiful jewelry box out of kitchen matches. Then he sent her a picture of himself, taken in prison, smiling. On the edge he wrote, "I'll love you forever."

One day, she wrote a letter to prison officials, asking for permission for her and Billy Joe to get married for the third time.

EPILOGUE

HERBERT Dale Biddle, Jr., the banker whose embezzlements caused Marjorie Jackson to withdraw her money, pleaded guilty to two counts of an eleven-count federal indictment. His original sentence of ten years in prison was reduced to two concurrent three-year terms. He became a model prisoner. Cited for trustworthiness, dependability and the need for only minor supervision, he completed a self-image seminar and a course in better living. Released after two and a half years, he got a job selling sporting goods equipment. He was thirty-seven.

Doug Green and Wally Bergin, Jr., pleaded guilty to conspiracy and were sentenced to two to fourteen years. The judge recommended both young men be allowed to serve their time in a youth facility or under a work-release program. Green also pleaded guilty to confinement; his sentence was made concurrent with the other sentence. The charge against Bergin was dropped.

Walter Bergin, Sr. received a suspended sentence. Placed on probation, he returned to Louisville, where he worked repairing small appliances.

The charge against Wally's sister Maywin was dropped.

No charges were filed against Gary Walters. He went to California, where he tried to raise $23 million for a movie about flying saucers. He told potential investors that he had invented a workable model of a flying saucer. The movie never was made.

Jerry Hornick received a suspended sentence.

Randy and Judy Parrish received suspended sentences.

No charges were filed against Ralph Wadsworth II. Authorities never identified "Dick Schakel" or the "some kid" who had gone on forays to the Jackson house.

Gary Perkins received a suspended sentence.

In 1979, the sheriff's department received an anonymous tip, from a woman, identifying Donald Earl Jones, thirty-three, Indianapolis, as one of the men who robbed Doug and Donna Green in their apartment. Jones identified his accomplices as truck driver Lowell Gilliland, twenty-six, a casual friend of Green's, and Bernard Egelhof, thirty-six. Jones said they escaped with about $100,000. Gilliland, who had waited outside, said the amount was closer to $70,000. Jones and Gilliland received suspended sentences. Egelhof, arrested in Texas, fought the case and was sentenced to one to ten years in prison.

Charges against John Alton Williams were reduced. He received a suspended sentence. So did Annie Young.

Emanuel Lee Robinson appealed his convictions unsuccessfully. Despite his claim of having $1,000,000 hidden, he pleaded poverty. Released in 1988, he was arrested in 1990 for burglary and sentenced to a ten-year term. He told the author in 1999 that he believed law enforcement officials had pocketed about $450,000 in cash.

Following her release from prison, Robertina Harroll returned to her home in Georgia. To make ends meet she stuffed pillows and bought knickknacks at flea markets for resale.

Correction authorities eventually approved Marjorie Pollitt's request to remarry Howard Willard.

Willard died, of heart disease, while jogging in the yard of the Indiana State Reformatory in 1987, age forty-eight. Marjorie arranged for his burial, next to his long-dead brother, in a Mooresville cemetery.

Agents of the Jackson estate sued twenty-five persons to recover money or merchandise they received through robberies of the home. Most were settled; a few were dismissed.

Marjorie Jackson's half-sister Roberta was named sole heir. After taxes and expenses, the assets were set at $9,578,282. She renounced half in favor of her six living children. An equal share went to the estate of a daughter killed in a traffic accident.

The house on Spring Mill Road was sold at auction for $51,500. The structure had been damaged badly by the fire. For a few years the property was a kind of tourist attraction, and, over time, it had a succession of owners.

Various investigations recovered a total of $3,720,000 from the burglary perpetrated by Willard and Robinson. Yet no one could say how much Jackson money remained unaccounted for. Some authorities were convinced substantial sums had been stolen without a trace.

Marjorie had withdrawn $7,880,000 in cash. Legal actions account for $8,500,000. But how much had been in the house to begin with? What of the perhaps $2,000,000 Chester had brought into the house around 1964 from his safe deposit box? How much cash had he squirreled away *before* then?

How many thefts or burglaries had been committed which Marjorie refused to acknowledge and never reported?

The answers went into the grave.

In a section of Crown Hill Cemetery in Indianapolis, Chester is buried near his murdered father, L.A. Jackson. Under a simple marker, his murdered wife is laid to rest on his right. Towering above the family plot of eight graves is a tall stone obelisk embellished with stone flowers, the embossed initials LAJ on each side, and, facing the tombs and monuments to the south, a single ill-fated name: JACKSON.

ACKNOWLEDGEMENTS

Most of the material in *Scavengers* is based on official records, interviews and transcripts, including, of course, trial testimony. The author thanks the numerous people who patiently answered questions, especially retired deputy Dave Paschall and attorney Robert C. Thompson, Jr. For insights, special thanks also to attorney Forrest B. Bowman, Jr.

Dick Cady won a Pulitzer Prize as the head of the Indianapolis Star's investigative team. He also worked for the Detroit News and Newsday. He is the author of "The Executioner's Mask" and "Champions," novels, and a memoir, "Deadline: Indianapolis."